CHINA IN CRISIS

The Role of the Military

Published by Jane's Defence Data
a division of Jane's Information Group Limited
"Jane's" is a Registered Trade Mark

Printed in the United Kingdom
ISBN 0-7106-0596-X

Jane's Information Group Limited
Sentinel House
163 Brighton Road
Coulsdon
Surrey CR3 2NX
United Kingdom

ISBN 0-7106-0596-X

Distributed in the Philippines and the USA and its dependencies by Jane's Information Group Inc, 1340 Braddock Place, Suite 300, PO Box 1436, Alexandria, Virginia 22313- 2036.

Typeset by
Laser Typesetting Services Limited, Laser House, Ockley Road, Croydon, CR0 3HP.

Printed and bound by Butler & Tanner, Frome, Somerset, United Kingdom

Contents

Introduction

The world was stunned by the events in Tiananmen Square in early June. In the West, the crushing of a relatively peaceful pro-democracy demonstration by seasoned troops — killing women, children, doctors, nurses — was unexpected. But it shouldn't have been so.

Using its worldwide network of correspondents, and contacts, as well as in-house resources, Jane's Information Group has established that the actions of the 27th Group Army should have been expected. It is not the first time that the People's Liberation Army has been used to crack down upon the civilian population. And it probably won't be the last.

This book reflects on the way in which the Old Guard reached the top of the People's Liberation Army through political position and influence rather than through military skills. Many have been waiting for this chance to show that they are still needed to defend the Party and the status quo. It has been impossible to split down the Group Armies and their commanders into political groupings, but rather we have found that personal position and relationships (including family ties) have been responsible for the events in Tiananmen Square. Even so, our contributors have chosen to use terms like 'more liberal' when the occasion justifies and the less violent approach of certain PLA formations.

We have also found evidence of a large number of favours being called in by the veterans of the Long March who have found it so much easier to crack down on 'counter-revolutionaries' than the younger, better trained (in Western eyes) commanders.

To try and understand this phenomenon, this book looks behind the scenes at the role of the PLA in Tiananmen Square, describes the background to the events by examining the history, philosophy, politics, personalities, rank structure and order of battle of the PLA.

In this book, we have endeavoured to present a factual account of the events in May and June 1989. To describe and analyse those events and place them into a wider context, particularly in respect of China's neighbours. We have drawn on a multitude of sources, using the talents of widely respected China watchers and commentators like Clare Hollingworth, Gerald Segal and G Jacobs. We have included a graphic account of the fateful night of 3/4 June from Jonathan Mirsky of *The Observer* newspaper which cannot fail to shock. We make no apology for such dramatic writing because dramatic events generate emotions which are relevant if put into the correct context.

The in-house specialist team at Jane's would like to thank all who have assisted with producing this special study in record time. As the events unfolded day-by-day, it became obvious to us that the situation needed to be accurately recorded and anaylsed. We hope that *CHINA IN CRISIS : The Role of the Military* is a credible document.

Paul Beaver   **June 1989**
Managing Editor
Jane's Defence Data

Contributors

Paul Beaver is Managing Editor, Jane's Defence Data. He lists Asian geo-politics amongst his specialist interests and has broadcast on television and radio about the recent events in China.

Henry Dodds is Editor, *Jane's Soviet Intelligence Review* with a special knowledge of orders of battle and military inventories. Henry has also broadcast on the background to Tiananmen Square and the People's Liberation Army in general.

Bridget Harney joined Jane's Defence Data as an editor from London University's School of Oriental and African Studies, where her main field was international relations which included Chinese affairs.

Clare Hollingworth is a well respected journalist and China Watcher with a detailed knowledge of events in the country. She lives and works in Hong Kong from where she has contributed on the Martial Law declaration and its consequences.

G Jacobs is a US-based China Watcher and Pacific Rim specialist with a detailed knowledge of current realities and future position of the People's Liberation Army.

Jonathan Mirsky was an eyewitness to the events in Tiananmen Square and sustained injuries which he received trying to record the events there. He is the China Specialist for *The Observer*, one of the United Kingdom's leading Sunday newspapers.

Stephen Prendergast studied Asia and Pacific Studies at Victoria University, Wellington (New Zealand), making China his specialist area. He first visited the country in 1975 and returned from his most recent visit to Beijing in January 1989.

Gerald Segal is a Research Fellow at the Royal Institute of International Affairs, London. He is also a Reader in International Politics at the University of Bristol (UK) and Editor of *The Pacific Review*.

Ian Tandy is an assistant editor at Jane's Defence Data, currently preparing an appointments and procurement guide to South East Asian nations.

Stuart Slade is a defence analyst with Jane's Information Group and a specialist in South East Asian affairs. He has travelled widely in the region.

Richard Woff is editor of *Soviet High Command* and *Warsaw Pact High Command* with a special knowledge of affairs relevant to the Soviet Union.

Marie Rowland is production supervisor for Jane's Information Group and has provided design and page layout expertise.

Kelly Davis is a secretary at Jane's Information Group and provided word processing support.

"The People's Liberation Army belongs to the people. It cannot confront the people. The army cannot enter the city." So wrote seven senior military officers in a letter in the People's Daily *on 22 May. On 5 June, two days after the massacre in Tiananmen Square, these tanks were photographed in Beijing.*

Tiananmen Square — an eyewitness recalls

**Jonathan Mirsky, *The Observer* newspaper's China specialist
has written this moving account:**

But do we learn then, as we secretly feared in our racist youth, that the Chinese are unusually cruel rat eaters who slide bamboo under fingernails, kill with a thousand cuts or with countless drip of water? Are their leaders, as a British diplomat said recently, just a bunch of thugs, who sometimes murder in the dark, one by one, or in the daylight in heaps which are then stacked up in hospital morgues or burned secretly at night?

There are such Chinese. They gave the orders for the Saturday night massacre. They drove the tanks which clanked over the students in Tiananmen, they fired the AK-47s which knocked over the doctors and nurses, and they tortured the wounded and bound students.

Such men are intellectual terrorists, too, who wish to crush the intellects and curiosity of the dissidents, like Professor Su Shaozhi, the purged director of the Marx-Lenin-Mao Zedong Thought Institute, who accused them of being Stalinist, and Fang Lizhi who dismisses Marx-Leninism as 'trivial' and suggests that nothing will change in China until 'the old men die.'

But then there are the non-cruel Chinese, the great mass. These have emerged during the last months as politically sensitive and in their great numbers so non-violently disciplined that they could have been trained by the Quakers. They brought into Tiananmen the statue of Liberty and the Goddess of Freedom, explaining that whereas the Statue of Liberty holds her torch with one hand, the defence of freedom in China is tougher and therefore requires two.

There were members of the Autonomous Workers Federation, in their tents in the Square — almost the first over which the tanks rolled — who made hundreds of people laugh with their comic dialogues between Mao and Deng meeting in Heaven. There were the doctors and nurses who piled out of the ambulance last Sunday morning on Changan Avenue, after the soldiers had shot down the parents of people who had been killed in the Square a few hours before, as they knelt among the dead and dying.

There were other doctors who risked immediate execution for permitting the BBC to bring its cameras into a hospital morgue or to see the piles of dead. And there were people who had tried to persuade me to leave Tiananmen Square when the soldiers began firing at us, and patted me kindly after the police had slugged me half senseless with their truncheons.

Finally, there is the singer from Taiwan, Hou Jedian, a pop idol in Beijing, and very rich, who came to Tiananmen Square to start a hunger strike with three companions. He had composed a song about the protests which he taught the crowd and which it rapturously sang.

He also composed a statement, which I had listened to him discuss at dinner. It said that he was coming to the Martyrs' Memorial to show the Li Peng Government that the Chinese had for too long listened and not spoken; that it was not a small handful opposing the regime, but the people themselves; and that Hou and his comrade were giving up food not for death but for life.

Hou was lucky to escape at the last moment as the soldiers charged toward the memorial. But it is true, none the less, that what happened in Tiananmen Square, beginning in mid-April and continuing until the massacre, was indeed for, life. This is what the old men could not stand, and it is why they will continue to attempt to snuff it out in the dark period ahead.

Untold thousands died in Tiananmen Square when troops moved in on the night of Saturday 3 June. Many were shot; some were crushed by tanks and armoured personnel carriers.

The Revenge of the Old Guard

Early on, when the student demonstrations started in Tiananmen Square in late April, the Chinese state propaganda machine rumbled into action. Loudspeakers boomed out over the vast and echoing square. The oration continued even as the tanks and armoured personnel carriers were crushing the demonstrators and their tents in the square and as soldiers fired indiscriminately into the crowd on 3 and 4 June. As the students erected the 10 metre-high Goddess of Liberty so that she faced Mao Zedong's portrait on the Gate of Heavenly Peace, the voice howled, "Your movement is bound to fail. It is foreign. This is China, not America." "The People's Liberation Army loves the people. The people loves the PLA. Only bad people do not love the Army."

In fact, the Chinese had loved the PLA. Everywhere children wore miniature imitations of its uniforms, and even when the troops tried to break into the city in their lorries, the crowds around their lorries were genuinely shocked. "How can you do this to us, do you have no shame, you are too young to shave, what were you going to do with your guns", they screamed at the sheepish men in the trucks.

On the Friday night before the Saturday massacre when thousands of poorly uniformed (indeed some were not in uniform at all) young soldiers came

On the morning of 3 June, Chinese army troops from the party headquarters garrison jogged through Beijing in a show of strength. Earlier, tens of thousands of troops marching towards Tiananmen Square had been turned back by huge crowds.

trotting down Changan Avenue, a few hundred metres from the square, they were surrounded by sleepy Beijing people in their underpants and pyjamas, who stripped them of their packs, scattered the meagre contents on the pavement, and scolded them for hours.

But there was no indication these young boys felt in any way threatened by the people.

Indeed, even after the great killing had begun, and the extent of the atrocity was known, people for the most part exercised restraint. Although some APC drivers who had run over pedestrians and soldiers who had shot children were set upon and killed by the crowd, most of those surrounded in their lorries, who had not yet used their guns, were not dragged out and killed, but remained the target of outrage and moral exhortation. Little wonder they often burned their own vehicles or offered their assault weapons to the crowd.

A question that will remain interminably on the lips of all those involved in the terrible events of 3/4 June will be why did the senior leaders Deng Xiaoping and President Yang Shangkun, order the massacre of students involved in non-violent demonstrations for liberalisation and democracy within the Chinese system?

It was possible that the 27th Group Army blasting its way through the road-blocks west of Tiananmen, crashing into the Square, and showering everyone in it with semi-automatic and machine gun fire, truly believed that the figures it saw moving about in the smoke and flame were not students and

Pro-democracy protesters link arms to hold back angry crowds from chasing a retreating group of soldiers near the Great Hall of the People on the morning of 3 June.

Jubilant students on top of an armoured personnel carrier they put out of action early in the morning of 4 June.

Chinese troops keep a sharp eye out as their truck makes a momentary stop on Changan Avenue.

working people, but those described on the official radio: *liu-mang* or hoodlums, combined with bad elements, reactionaries, class enemies and counter-revolutionaries, who were intent on overthrowing the Government, the Party, the State and Communism itself.

To soldiers from remote units kept away from radios (on which they might hear the BBC World Service) and from newspapers which had begun printing from too-subtly coded articles supporting the protest, shooting the moving figures in the Square might have seemed their patriotic and military duty.

But what seems so inexplicable is why the soldiers continued to shoot the next day. Frantic parents of those who had been gunned down and bayoneted the night before (many of whose bodies would never be found — hastily burned by the army) clustered around the roadblock in front of the Beijing Hotel, a couple of hundred yards from the square. Even here the soldiers had seemed unable to restrain themselves and orders were given to shoot. Many were killed and wounded. The doctors and nurses who poured out of the ambulances arriving at the scene also lay, moments later, with those they had come to help.

How could all this have happened? Deng, Yang and others around them, except for Premier Li Peng, suffered at Mao Zedong's hands during the Cultural Revolution, lost comrades and relatives (one of Deng's sons was thrown from a window and paralysed for life). They bitterly condemn the years 1966-1976 as the greatest tragedy China has suffered in modern times.

Deng, most believed, was a man devoted to the modernisation of China. So devoid of ideological commitment that he is attributed with saying, "Who cares what colour a cat is as long as it

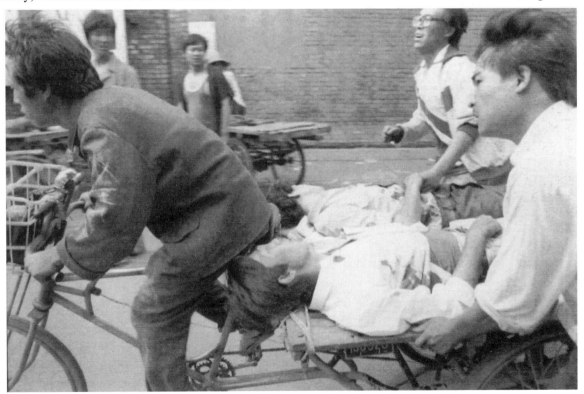

A rickshaw carrying wounded is pedalled frantically to a nearby hospital on 4 June after troops fired hundreds of rounds towards angry crowds gathered outside Tiananmen Square at noon.

catches mice?" (During the days before the massacre, posters had appeared in and around Tiananmen Square saying 'Who cares what colour our cat is as long as it resigns'). He was the man who had shaken hands with British prime minister Margaret Thatcher and the Queen and who was hailed as the originator of the Hong Kong settlement formula. One country, two systems, intended to assure the inhabitants of that territory that their future was safe in Beijing's hands.

The conviction that the Party and the Party alone stands between the Chinese people and *luan* (chaos), is the key to Deng's character and to the bloodshed of early June. From his resumption of power after Mao's death and the arrest of the 'Gang of Four' in late 1976, Deng planned and ordered the Four Modernisations in agriculture, industry, defence and science to attain *fu-quiang*

— wealth and power-through quadrupled production by the year 2000. But he also regularly suppressed anything that looked like a challenge to the Party supremacy.

In 1979-80, hundreds of pamphleteers were arrested for their activities around Democracy Wall, where the now imprisoned Wei Jingsheng called for a fifth modernisation — democracy. Thereafter in successive drives against spiritual pollution and bourgeois liberalisation, Deng showed where his priorities really lay, on one occasion, he warned young leaders against the appearance in China of anything that resembled Solidarity (the Polish free trade union), and during the summit with Mikhail Gorbachov he showed no enthusiasm for Soviet-style political reform.

Most telling of all, Deng confessed, according to a recent speech by Yang Shangkun, that the two

Dead bodies, pictured on 5 June, lie in a makeshift morgue at the Post and Telecommunications Hospital in western Beijing. (Photograph: David Turnley)

greatest mistakes of his life were the appointments as Party General Secretary, of Hu Yaobang and Zhao Ziyang. In 1987, Deng forced Hu's resignation for failing to stop campus demonstrations for more democracy and threatening to expose high-level corruption.

At some point in late May Deng moved again, to remove Zhao Ziyang — also for encouraging dissenting students, admitting that his own sons were corrupt, and daring to disagree with the Supreme Leader on whether the students were hoodlums and traitors. Only this time Zhao refused to go quietly, like Hu, and had to be forcibly removed from the scene. He was certainly placed under arrest and perhaps even killed.

Zhao's supporters and disciples, especially those in the four Institutes that acted as thinktanks, were soon being 'investigated' as counter-revolutionaries, a deeply serious crime in China. As the murderous days dragged on, they too faced imprisonment and perhaps execution.

Deng quickly made common cause with what appeared at first glance like an unlikely group of ancient allies. In addition to Yang Shangkun, 82, there was Chen Yun, 84, Wang Zhen, 81, Peng Zhen, 87, and Li Xiannian, 80. These octogenarians, who once held the highest party and government posts, with the exception of Yang, had been gently retired a few years before because they were convinced that the economic reforms encouraging individual initiative, initiated by Deng and steered along by Hu and Zhao, would destroy central control, and were encouraging the spiritually polluting ideas of Western-style democracy and bourgeois liberalism.

Deng may have had a weakness for economic decentralisation. But when the mourning for Hu blossomed into popular demands for democracy, dialogue between the leaders and organisations not chosen by them, and ultimately for the resignation of Li Peng, Yang Shangkun, and Deng himself, Deng agreed with the old comrades on the importance of total political control.

After they had delivered speeches damning

By 10 June, a week after the massacre, troops had firmly re-established control in Tiananmen Square, even to the extent of placing tanks and armed guards at the entrance to the Forbidden City.

Western-style democracy, and had even warned Deng, in an only slightly coded fashion, against the further exercise of personal rather than collective leadership, Deng knew he could count on them for tough action against the protests. Nonetheless, Deng may have underestimated Yang Shangkun's own ambitions to succeed him in any succession struggle. Such action became increasingly important once the soldiers had been turned back non-violently by citizens from their real task which was not to crush the students but to secure Beijing against a possible counter-coup by the followers of Zhao Ziyang.

Yang is as deeply committed as Deng. He is known to have insisted on the removal of Hu Yaobang in December 1986 and to have opposed Zhao as his successor. Yang has familial ties with the 27th Group Army, and it was he who had ensured that it was isolated from news of the demonstrations in Tianaman Square.

As for Chen Yun, Li Xiannian, Peng Zhen and the rest of the aged gang, while they may not have approved the mass killing of 3/4 June, their speeches, in which words, like counter-revolutionary, danger to the state and to the Party, were freely used together with charges of conspiracy, created an atmosphere of emergency and alarm which could have been used to fire up the PLA for the job they were given in the Square.

These old men, palsied as they sometimes are, staring vacantly into space during televised broadcasts, sometimes supported by nurses and unable to give speech without losing their place in the text, are convinced of one thing: they are the Founding Members of The Firm. 'We entered the party 60 years ago', they reminded one another, 'we survived the Long March in 1935, the Japanese, Chiang Kai-shek, the early years of land reforms — when we killed hundreds of thousands of land-lords and class enemies. We endured Mao's Cultural Revolution, which hundreds in the Politburo, the Central Committee and the High Command did not survive. This is our country and our Party and no one is going to take it from us, certainly not that rabble in the square, provoked and misled by Zhao Ziyang.'

It is this attitude which explains the rumours running through Beijing in late May that Deng had said, "Two hundred thousand deaths are not too many to ensure 20 years of stability," and "What are a million deaths in a population of one billion?"

There was little evidence to suggest that some of the guilt-stricken units, even the 38th Group Army, whose commander appears to have been removed for failing to march into Beijing on the 20 May because his daughter was a student there, might turn on the worst perpetrators of the horrors — the 27th Group Army. Chinese commanders, although divided into semi-autonomous regions, are ultimately feudal in outlook, and if they believe the old Hero's of the Revolution are behind what is going on, they will take their orders, although they may modify them where possible.

Martial Law in Beijing Causes and Consequences

Beijing Radio announced during the evening of Friday, 19 May that Martial Law would be enforced in Tiananmen Square and the city centre from 10am the following morning.

Premier Li Peng, as Chairman of the State Council, was responsible for the proclamation that meant students and their supporters would be removed from the Square — the place where they had encamped as a base for demonstrations demanding more democracy and press freedom. On hearing of the proclamation, the students and their supporters from amongst the workers, who were well organised, established barricades on the main routes into the city.

Buses, lorries and cars were lined up across main roads at intervals of around a hundred metres and manned by students who allowed private citizens and trucks carrying food to pass. But when troops arrived from the 38th Group Army they were surrounded by students shouting: "You are the People's Army; you cannot act against the People". The soldiers, who were generally unarmed, turned their vehicles round and, still surrounded by students re-enforced with workers,

On the morning of 20 May, the day martial law was due to take effect, soldiers wave from a truck as it is turned back from the city centre at a roadblock manned by students.

they were then lectured on the virtues and advantages of democracy. After a few hours, the troops, many of whom came from the area round the capital, were fraternising with the locals. None reached the Square although a company that arrived by train were within a kilometre and a half before being turned back by students and made to sit in railway carriages on Platform 6.

Martial Law re-awakened lagging enthusiasm and support for the students and workers as demonstrators marched to the Square shouting and carrying large banners demanding "Crush Li Peng" or "Hang Li Peng" while others said "Thanks Deng but its time to say 'Bye Bye'." Over a million people filled the Square and the battalion of troops, normally based in buildings in the old Legation quarter nearby, did not show their faces. The crowds included off-duty soldiers, officials, journalists as well as bank clerks and members of the business community. Money was collected to provide food for the students sleeping in miserable conditions on the Square who announced they would remain there until the National People's Congress (China's Parliament) met on 20 June.

The man to whom Deng Xiaoping had handed the day to day administration of the PLA, Zhao Ziyang, played no role in the proclamation of Martial Law or its enforcement. His place, as Executive Vice Chairman, was taken by the State President, Yang Shangkun (81), who had already been active in supporting his brother, Yang Baibing, (Director of the General Political Department of the PLA and in charge of Political Commissars), in re-instating their role as instructors of 'political thought'. General Qin Jiwei, the Minister of Defence, did not appear at his desk after Martial Law was proclaimed nor did some thirty senior officials. Indeed, the administration so far as Ministries were concerned appeared to cease to function but, to be fair, apart from some minor

On the 22 May, the Chinese authorities used an army Gazelle helicopter to drop leaflets to students in Tiananmen Square, warning them to abandon the Square or be forced out by the military.

food shortages and lack of petrol, life appeared normal in streets where there were no demonstrations. However, one ministry — the Finance Ministry — did not stay closed for long and within two weeks of the massacre in Tiananmen Square was functioning normally, even to the extent of signing contracts with Hong Kong firms.

Until Martial Law the students had been fortunate. There had been unrest on the campuses since the death of Hu Yaobang on 15 April, as students and professors alike criticised Deng Xiaoping for having dismissed him earlier as Party Secretary. They felt secure in the belief that no action would be taken against them as the Government prepared for the Summit meeting with the Soviet leader, Mikhail Gorbachev in mid-May. Indeed, the students used the press and television teams assembled to cover the Summit to gain global publicity for their cause. Martial Law was planned and directed from a new underground military headquarters, believed to be some two miles to the west of Zhongnanhai where members of the ruling Politburo normally live and work in the west of the Forbidden City. The soldiers and politicians went to their new headquarters by a secret underground route.

While the Summit was taking place units of the 38th Group Army were camping in fields in the south of the city as well as in disused factories and hospitals. Whenever possible the soldiers appeared to be fraternising with the local population. Experts noted that, although the 38th has always been known as the most modern and well equipped of the Group Armies, the armoured personnel carriers (APCs) it was equipped with had obviously been in storage for some years, indeed, in some cases,

Seen before the events of 3/4 June brought the protest in Tiananmen Square to a tragic conclusion, a pro-democracy demonstrator signals victory to the crowds as troops withdraw on the west side of the Great Hall of the People.

Armed police officers on duty in Tiananmen Square before the declaration of martial law.

the tarpaulin covering the machine guns had stuck to the barrels.

Some days before the Soviet party arrived, President Yang Shangkun gave orders to his brother

that when the troops were 'camping' beyond the suburbs as they encircled Beijing, they should receive at least four hours daily indoctrination on the situation as seen by the radical 'hardliners', and on the vital issue of clearing the Square of students and workers. Many units thus received up to two weeks of lectures and study. 'Study' is the PLA euphemism for political indoctrination and in the days of the late Chairman Mao Zedong not only did the troops have an hour's study each day but a Political Commissar was appointed to every unit of company size (approximately 130 men) or above. The Commissar marched with the men, ate with them and shared their recreation. Thus any soldier who expressed views not compatible with the 'Party Line' was reprimanded.

The modernisation programme, however, reduced the status of the Commissar as there was no room for non-combatants in a tank, APC or truck. Further, the troops were too busy learning how to repair tank engines or operate new communications equipment to devote time to

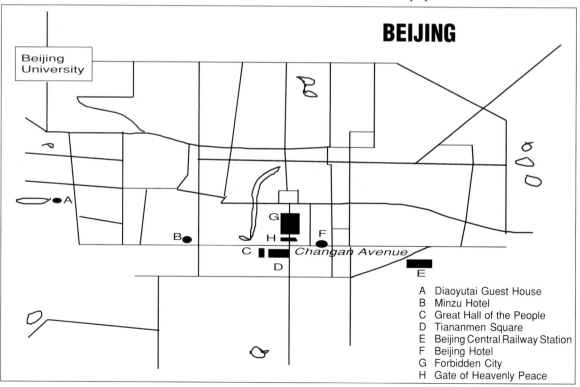

A Diaoyutai Guest House
B Minzu Hotel
C Great Hall of the People
D Tiananmen Square
E Beijing Central Railway Station
F Beijing Hotel
G Forbidden City
H Gate of Heavenly Peace

Chinese troops sealing off one of the diplomatic compounds in reaction to suspected sniper fire.

Crowds of bravely curious Beijing residents gather to look at the military hardware in Tiananmen Square.

'study' and the daily session became a weekly one until Yang's orders were received.

As Deng Xiaoping had lost the support of Zhao Ziyang and the reformists he was dependent on the party elders, all in their eighties who came out of retirement to assist him. They included Chen Yun, Li Xiannian, Peng Zhen, Wang Zhen and 'Big Sister Deng Yingchao', widow of the late Premier Zhou Enlai. They all took part in the Long March and are convinced believers in 'Marx, Lenin and Mao Zedong thought'. The 'oldies' as they are dubbed, rallied support for Deng in the provinces amongst the 'hardliners' as diplomats realised the students had brought the power struggle — who will take over after Deng — into the open. Earlier it had been assumed Zhao Ziyang, who is both a political and economic reformist and believes in opening the door still further to the west, would take over later this year when Deng Xiaoping is

expected to resign from his last remaining post, that of Chairman of the Military Affairs Commission. There will be bitter in-fighting on who takes over this vital post with responsibility for the Defence forces and the finger on the nuclear trigger.

There were fears of civil war amongst the population as they witnessed soldiers on friendly terms with the inhabitants of the outer suburbs of Beijing while reports were reaching the Capital of massive troops movements towards the city throughout the vast country.

Deng Xiaoping was falsely reported to fly to Wunan, where early summer manoeuvres were taking place, to talk with the Regional Military Commanders and Group Army Commanders. In fact, they came to see him in the Capital as plans were discussed for the encirclement of Beijing by armed troops and a final move into the city to clear

A Chinese family on a bicycle, including a small child, ride in front of a column of troops.

the Square.

The seven Regional Commanders all made public statements of support for Deng, which is not surprising considering they were all appointed by him as 'his' men. Deng was careful not to risk a military *coup d'etat* similar to the one organised by the late Chairman's right hand man Lin Biao. Thus, the Regional Commanders are frequently called 'grey' and they do appear to have less real authority today than the younger commanders of the new Group Armies.

Deng decided around 1980 there would be no global war this century and that it was, therefore, the ideal moment to begin the modernisation and streamlining of the PLA. This involved, so far as the land forces are concerned, the transformation of 36 (Maoist) Field Armies into 22 or 24 mobile and supposedly fully integrated Group Armies.

There is no standardisation in the structure of the Group Armies but all, when fully equipped, will have integral battlefield air support and those near the sea or a major river will include naval units. Some of the proposed 22 Group Armies only exist on paper whilst others have trucks but lack modern communications equipment and are short of field artillery and APCs. The PLA has already been cut by well over a million men and women (between 1987-89) and it was expected that Zhao Ziyang would make further reductions next year (1990) especially amongst the Political Commissars. Some Group Armies complain that their most modern and fastest equipment has been taken away from them in order to arm the Quick Reaction Forces that Deng was keen to form in case of sudden border problems with Vietnam.

After the failure of the 38th Group Army, Yang

Deng Xiaoping shakes hands, on 9 June, with PLA officers while former president Li Xiannian, left, looks on. Deng praised the military suppression of the pro-democracy movement.

Shangkun supported by Deng made detailed plans for Group Armies from distant parts to be deployed around Peking. Passenger trains were cancelled, together with domestic air flights, as the 27th Group Army made its way from Shijiazhuang followed by major units from the 38th and 39th from Shenyang, the 15th Airborne from Wuhan together with elements of the 54th from Jinan, the 14th from Sichuan, the 24th from Chengde, Inner Mongolia and the 1st and 12th from Nanjing. The 6th Tank division normally deployed in Beijing was considered to be loyal to the 'hardliners' and the 1st Tank Division normally deployed in Tiajin was moved to the capital in support.

The following Group Armies were apparently of "uncertain loyalty": the 16th and 40th now in Shenyang and the 28th, 63rd and 67th whose current whereabouts are unknown. There were, too, problems with the People's Liberation Army Air Force. Deng and Yang however, persuaded the men that economic reforms would continue and it was "bad elements and counter revolutionaries" who had persuaded the students and workers to cause so much trouble. Morale was raised when General Qin Jiwei, the Defence Minister, belatedly gave his support to Deng by appearing with the troops about to enter the capital.

Millions around the world have seen on television the 27th Group Army smashing its way into the Square putting an end to the occupation by students and workers. Tanks supported the 27th not only in the Square but on a series of bridges that overlook one of the diplomatic compounds and office blocks occupied by foreigners. A week after the onslaught elements of the 27th, 39th, 24th and 28th Group Armies were occupying the Square and important cross roads in the city. There were, too, suggestions that a company from the 38th had also been seen. There have been no confirmed reports of skirmishes

between elements in the PLA supporting the 'hardliners' and those in favour of the reformists that were forecast so confidently at the time civil war was also feared.

Shortly after the 27th Group Army took over the Square, students and those workers who were members of what is now called an "illegal trade union" went into hiding. In mid-June a major purge was still in progress.

Although the Ministry of Foreign Affairs has nothing to say to foreign embassies in Beijing, officials everywhere are back at their desks with the exception of the few in hiding. The Chinese are anxiously awaiting a meeting of the Central Committee of the Communist Party to endorse, amongst other items, the resignation of Zhao Ziyang as Secretary-General of the Party and Vice Chairman of the Military Affairs Commission. Considerable surprise has been expressed that the meeting has been delayed for so long as it is thought unlikely Martial Law will not be lifted until the new appointments are officially announced.

'Many' senior Commanders are officially reported to have been 'dismissed' due to their uncertain loyalty before the 27th Army Group moved into the Square. The 27th was, it is officially stated, supported by units — some small — from all seven Military Regions.

It is expected that Qiao Shi (65) will take over as Secretary General. He is a member of the five man Standing Committee of the Politburo and has been in charge of state security. President Yang Shangkun (80) will become the Vice Chairman of the Military Affairs Commission and continue to be responsible for the day to day administration of the PLA. There are many indications that the power struggle in Beijing continues.

Beijing commuters, in sparse numbers, ride bicycles under an overpass guarded by a tank. The slogan on the wall on the left reads 'strike down martial law.'

Role of the PLA in Tiananmen Square

The violent end to the peaceful democracy movement's rally in Tiananmen Square shocked a world which had been expecting a peaceful revolution. The students gathered in the very centre of Beijing's autocratic past, the Forbidden City, had already succeeded in changing the programme of the first Sino-Soviet meeting for 30 years. Even in the west, the historical nature of the Deng-Gorbachev meeting was overshadowed by the actions of what the Old Guard were later to call 'counter-revolutionaries.'

That same Old Guard of the ruling Communist Party could not be expected — with hindsight — to allow this challenge to Party rule to go unpunished. But nobody really expected tanks, bullets and bayonets. The shock was even greater because the bloody crackdown was carried out by an army whose very title was directly associated with the support of the people.

The Martial Law declaration on 20 May, ordered by the Central Military Commission, relayed and published by the PLA General Staff Headquarters (Political and Logistic Department), demanded that the officers and men of all Martial Law Enforcement Forces "obey orders and take a clear-cut stand in fighting against a plot of very few people."

The continuing demonstrations between 27 April and 3 June undoubtedly reminded the Chinese leadership of those circumstances surrounding the famous 'Fourth of May Movement' (1919) and the Nanjing Uprising of 1 August 1927 which resulted in the establishment of their power base — the Chinese Communist Party. These events were followed by two decades of fighting for control of the Chinese mainland; Deng's contemporaries did not want to see their demise under similar conditions and soon came to the decision to apply military power.

Immediately before the massacre, including Saturday morning, the PLA had been mobilising troops from the provinces to replace elements of

As many as 150 000 soldiers were brought into Beijing by train and in trucks. Some of the early convoys — like this one of 200 trucks pictured on 21 May — were stopped before they could enter the city.

21

the more liberal Beijing Garrison. Initially, the 27th Group Army from Hebei Province, in the West (although it was originally thought the unit came from Shenyang, on the Sino-Soviet border) was moved up. The unit moved into the west of the capital city, taking up defensive positions on roof tops and behind walls in the area adjacent to the Forbidden City.

Other PLA units were brought into the City from four directions. According to reliable reports coming from Western intelligence agencies and widely quoted in newspapers and news reports from Canberra to London, massive army movement preceded the Tiananmen Square massacre. Sources indicate that as many as 150 000 soldiers were trucked and trained into Beijing. The employment of military forces, including the airborne and maritime elements of the PLA, to suppress or contain a people's uprising reflects the Chinese leadership's lack of confidence in the ability of the recently established People's Armed Police to maintain civil order or peaceful control of land, sea and air boundaries.

The military moved in. From Shenyang Province, the recently reformed 16th, 39th, 40th and 64th Group Armies, were brought into the city from their bases which are thought to include locations along the Sino-Soviet border.

The Chinese threat perception had, ironically, been recently changed following the summit meeting between Deng Xiaoping and Mikhail Gorbachev and the release of so many troops was not thought to constitute a risk to the nation's sovereignty. Quite the reverse, the 'counter-revolutionaries' in Tiananmen Square were thought to pose a far greater risk to the country, the Party and the positions so jealously guarded by the hardliners. At least two of the Group Armies from Shenyang are thought to have been under training in areas close to the North Korean border, but the exact locations of their depots remain unclear.

To the south, in Lanzhou Province, elements of

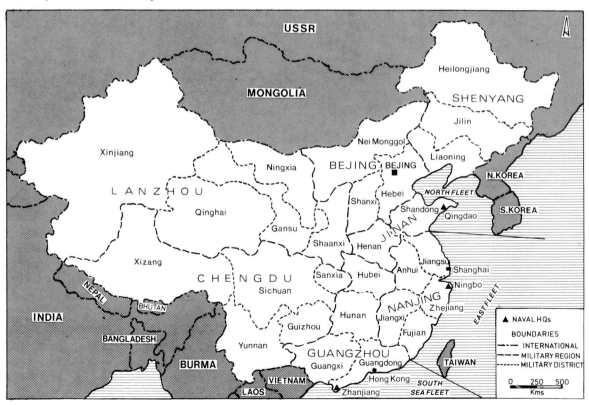

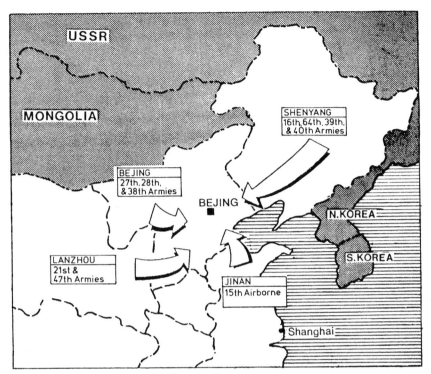

Some soldiers have even been accused of handing over personal weapons and material for making fire bombs to the students. This seems to be particularly difficult to confirm, especially because in China, the rules about the possession of personal weapons are very onerous to those to whom they have been issued. The loss of a rifle or pistol is a major disciplinary offence.

The mere fact that the 38th Group Army, known to local people as the Beijing Army, had been unsuccessful in its attempt to clear the Square of demonstrators had stretched the loyalties of the troops. In any case, it was reasoned by the Military Commission, chaired by Deng, that the effects of the Tiananmen demonstrations on army morale were alarming, both at the command level and among the other soldiers. There was a sense of humiliation.

Western observers, including intelligence agencies in surrounding nations, are convinced that the 38th represents the most professional and best-equipped element of the newly created Group Armies. In terms of hardline discipline, however, the 27th apparently rates higher.

This should be seen against the background of reports in the *People's Daily* in March which identified criminal elements within the PLA. The newspaper told its readers that the PLA, once the pride of the nation, had become a 'stupid army', the refuge for murderers, thieves, mentally unstable and generally unfit people.

The report was thought to have been placed in the newspaper at the start of the 1989 conscription induction to encourage a greater pride in army service. With the background of corrupt and exaggerated form-filling, the general impression

the 21st and 47th Group Armies were trucked into the southern outskirts of Beijing, although it is understood that they did not appear on the streets until after the massacre. The 15th Airborne Division, not thought to be one of the 22 newly created Integrated Group Armies were flown into Beijing from Wuhan Hubei Province, Guandong Military Region in seven or eight Boeing 757s of the Chinese national air carrier, CAAC.

The loyalty to the Old Guard of the Chinese Communist Party of the three major units within the Beijing military region and garrison area has been frequently questioned in the western media. It is certain that the 38th Group Army, which apparently moved into Beijing after martial law was declared on 20 May, had personal, ethnic, family and personal relationships with many of the students.

The Times newspaper even goes as far as to say, in its edition of 8 June, that many students in Tiananmen Square had completed their pre-university military service in the Group before going up to higher education.

'Counter-revolutionaries' in Tiananmen Square, as they were portrayed by the leadership, were thought to pose a far greater risk to the country than mobilising 150 000 troops.

feel the sense of humiliation on which the Old Guard were able to trust when the order was given to clear the Square.

There is no doubt that the decision to move in against the students was taken at the very top of the command structure, probably by Deng himself. To ensure co-ordination of effort, the negation of any risk of *coup d'etat* by a single unit with a dynamic leader and to reduce the risk of medium-high level power broking, command was undertaken by a general staff military committee.

Units pulled in from all over the country were widespread in disposition and origin to spread the guilt and to avoid future dissent rather than any reluctance to carry out orders by the 38th or 27th Group Armies.

Much of the troop movement during the Saturday night and Sunday was the deployment of soldiers

A PLA soldier gives a worried look at the angry crowd surrounding his unit on the west side of the Great Hall of the People. The crowd was angered by an earlier attack on students and civilians by troops using tear gas and truncheons.

has been that the quality of the average unit has been below par for several years.

Professional soldier entry has also suffered. Examples are often cited as a reflection of the modernisation programme which has required those with a technical background to operate new equipment. But for the would-be professional soldier there have been other opportunities in commerce and industry.

Does this mean that the soldiers being recruited are also those who, in the old English adage, are cannon fodder? Those capable of taking orders and carrying them through without a second thought. Such strong headed people — not really capable of thinking as individuals — would fully

One of two Chinese soldiers mans a light machine gun pointed towards a foreign diplomatic compound. (Photograph: David Turnley)

A company of PLA troops moves down Changan Avenue on 5 June, firing indiscriminately as they go.

A youth swings on the barrel of a disabled T-69 tank as others clamber over it.

rather than a concerted attempt to dislodge the hardline elements. This also includes activity surrounding Beijing in the days prior to the massacre. According to Chinese sources available to *Jane's Defence Data*, the replacement of troops and assembly of support equipment ran smoothly as less reliable units were replaced.

A Chinese source has advised that the PLA Air Force and Navy commanders, as early as mid May, had indicated their full support for Deng and Li Peng's decision to use overpowering weight of military force to quell what appeared to them to be the start of an organised national counter-revolution. The PLA Navy, ever since the early 1980s, particularly after Liu Huaqing became its third commander-in-chief has been a keen and constant supporter of Deng Xiaoping and the Chinese Communist Party leadership. Therefore, it should not be surprising to find the PLA Navy in the forefront of support for Party-directed actions as a means of promoting leadership adherence to its current force modernisation programme.

Presumably, this indication of full support further reinforced Li Peng's ultimate decision to employ military forces knowing that fleeing dissidents could most probably be contained within China's sovereign territory. The PLA Navy's role in this crisis has been to monitor and neutralise attempts of dissident exfiltration or infiltration of the coastal areas in co-ordination with seaborne elements of the People's Armed Police. Command and control functions of the Coastal Region Defence Forces are integrated with Border Guard and Sea Fleet surveillance detachments.

A truck load of PLA soldiers, part of a convoy of several hundred military vehicles, moves through Beijing.

Elements of the khaki-jacketed, blue-trousered 15th Airborne Division — a quick response force established in 1988 by the PLA Airborne Command — spearheaded the supression force's action in the Square. This force's baptism of fire was probably in Tibet in late 1988/early 1989 but it certainly demonstrated its ability to be deployed anywhere within China at short notice.

The aftermath of Tiananmen Square involves cover-up, exaggeration and the public propagation of lies. It also confirms the Mao Zedong perception that 'political power flows from the barrel of a gun.'

In the days before the massacre in Tiananmen Square, convoys of troops were stopped by students. The only action the students took against the troops was to offer them food, which was seen by senior army commanders as a humiliation.

It has been reported that several generals were removed from their posts before the imposition of Martial Law as being politically unreliable. There were other leaders — younger and older — willing and eager to take their places. While people in the streets of Beijing have held the 27th responsible for most of the atrocities, the troops involved have actually been drawn in from different units around the country. Accounts of disorder and rival factions within the armed forces appear to be highly exaggerated. The soldiers were moved in to Tiananmen Square to achieve total military control — which meant orders to kill must have been issued.

Those graphic television pictures of the first armoured personnel carrier stalled on a barrier and set alight suggests an act of provocation. The crew of that vehicle were men sent in as a sacrifice to enrage soldiers and consolidate their unity against students.

It is obvious that the number of troops killed has been exaggerated by the Chinese government, although it is obvious that some were killed. Those that lost their lives did so in the melée of Tiananmen Square with its echoes, darkness and confusion. There it was difficult to tell which direction shots were coming from and who was firing them.

From independent eyewitnesses and other reports in the media, quoted around the world and supported by government statements from many nations, it is obvious that civilian deaths and casualties far outweighed army casualties. The PLA Army suffered heavy equipment losses in terms of main battle tanks, armoured personnel carriers, and lorries with reports of as many as 100 trucks and associated support vehicles being set on fire. Reports have also indicated that many vehicles were burned by their own drivers.

Soldiers of the 27th Group Army did not have it all their own way. According to a fine art study group from Horley, Surrey in southern England, onlookers lynched a soldier who had indiscriminately killed three young girls. Needless to say, the girls were unarmed and had pleaded for their lives before the soldier emptied his Type 56 assault rifle's magazine into them. The soldier, before he was hung from a tree, had also shot an old man who tried to cross the street.

Students told western tourists fleeing the country that the soldiers were on amphetamines or other stimulant drugs. Apparently, according to the students, the soldiers had been told that there was an outbreak of measles in the Square following the weeks of squatting by local students. Certainly after seven weeks of occupation, the conditions were unsanitary but it seems unlikely that the troops were at any health risk.

Neither can there be any rational reason why the PLA needed to use armoured personnel carriers, main battle tanks and automatic weapons. The lack of internal security and crowd control training was very apparent — but equally so was the local commander's lack of regard for his fellow countrymen.

Many observers believe that this was as a direct result of the previous PLA experience. The fact that the 27th Group Army, unlike others formed under the recent modernisation plans, is made up of a greater ratio of professional enlistees to conscripted soldiers is also important in understanding the reaction of the soldiers.

The hardline hierarchy of the PLA was also dismayed at the soft approach of the local Beijing Garrison commander in the two days immediately before the massacre. According to reliable reports quoted in *Newsweek* magazine, other demonstrators, however, had also greeted some soldiers, probably unarmed, with stones and petrol bombs.

There is no doubt that initially the bulk of students peaceably resisted troop movements. They surrounded the troops, climbed on tanks, offered them food and argued with them. This whole turn of events was thoroughly humiliating for the army. Following regrouping and resupply they were then cut off from newspapers and radio reports for over ten days before they were ordered to forcibly impose Martial Law.

'Bad Iron' and Tiananmen

"Good iron does not make nails, good men do not make soldiers", says an ancient Chinese proverb. This characterisation, so-called 'bad iron', is given to soldiers by the people generally and by the officers who command them. However, characterising PLA soldiers as 'bad iron' will certainly be difficult for those senior PLA officers trying to implement modernisation and other reforms.

The struggle for democracy in China which began in April involves a traditional political power struggle among China's ageing autocrats.

In this struggle some senior members of the People's Liberation Army are pitted against those who wish the PLA to remain a 'non-political' professional army with main interests centred on modernisation of the armed forces. For all intents and purposes this process would be in line with modern Western armies. Others are 'crossing the institutional line' which has theoretically divided Army from Party and State and thus are not limiting their ambitions to the military world.

Caught literally in the middle, with such tragic results, were the idealistic university students and free trade union supporters of a new form of government who hoped to seize upon the

A cyclist rides warily past Chinese soldiers guarding an intersection in central Beijing a few days after troops cleared Tiananmen Square.

liberalising economic reforms of an ageing and at times infirm Deng Xiaoping. They wanted to institute political reforms that would transform traditional Chinese centralism and parochialism.

In many respects, the conditions are analogous to those in Taiwan during the period of 1965 to 1980. Following the death of Chiang Kai-shek, liberal economic reforms were instituted without matching political reforms as the 'old men' behind the Guomindang (Kuomintang) leadership strove to retain their formal titles, influence and privileges.

"The students and the Army have something in common," notes Dr J T Dreyer, a well-respected China watcher. "Both have been hurt very badly by Deng's free market reforms, which have caused a sharp rise in prices...this is even more of a problem for them than for other elements of Chinese society, because students and military people are on fixed incomes."

Most of the 38th Group Army's recruits were from Beijing, while those of the 27th were from outside the capital to the South; from rural areas where 'private farming' is now permitted, allowing for limited capitalism and profit taking. Additionally, in the absence of the ability to integrate advanced weapons into the PLA in recent years, the leadership of the Army has done the only thing possible towards modernising the force: increased training and emphasis on improved tactics, but this is no real alternative for high technology equipment. It is those same students who were killed in Tiananmen Square that are needed to operate the new systems.

The events in Beijing and in some other Chinese

One immediate effect of the PLA's actions will be a drastic loss of military technology from the West, as in this NVH-1 infantry fighting vehicle, a result of Sino-British co-operation.

cities have, however, brought a new prominence for the military. A number of China watchers have noted that political strife and internal factionalism among senior political figures ultimately results in expanded roles for the PLA in administering.

As one Hong Kong-based diplomat observed in May, "as soon as things stabilise, the military leaders may call a Chinese communist party Central Committee meeting and appoint a new leadership. The Army will say, "this is it, the game's over. This is the new leadership....and then they'll get around to rooting out the opposition one by one."

This observation clearly has some merit for the Army who has been uncomfortable with its current role in this leadership crisis. Signs are that this happened over the weekend of 17/18 June in a semi-secret meeting close to Beijing, doubtless to be followed by a purge.

Since 1985, the PLA has been in the process of a major demobilisation and re-organisation, and is clearly not trained or prepared for riot control duties as was vividly illustrated by the actions of the 27th Group Army. These were disciplined but peasant-minded troops from rural areas away from urbane Beijing, who in some respects may have felt some hostility towards the students and certainly had little understanding of their 'Democracy Movement'; in contrast to the 38th Group Army and People's Armed Police personnel stationed in Beijing from the beginning.

The degree of division within the Army is evident from the petition signed in the third week of May by about 100 military officers, drafted by seven retired generals (including a minister Zhang Aiping and Chief-of-Staff Yang Dezhi) urging restraint on the part of the Party in the emerging crisis. This petition was published in the *People's Daily* and is quoted under the Frontispiece of this book.

Whether Defence Minister, General Qin Jiwei and various Army level commanders can weather the current political storm with their positions intact remains to be seen.

For the PLA as a whole, there clearly will be short-term and long-term losses as a result of the current political struggle in Beijing.

In the short term these will include the drastic loss of military technology transfers from Western nations and immediate loss of the limited hardware transfers from the United States, United Kingdom, and others who have placed bans on military exports to China. President Bush and Prime Minister Margaret Thatcher were amongst the first foreign leaders to condemn the actions in Tiananmen Square.

In addition, the US administration has shown disquiet over the Fang Lizhi incident earlier this year when the dissident was prohibited from attending a dinner for George Bush in Beijing. There will now be increased diplomatic tensions as the US Embassy in Beijing shelters Fang Lizhi and this will undoubtedly spill over into the US perception of the PLA.

The bottom line will be a general slowing of the PLA's modernisation process, which ironically will not offend many of the Old Guard who still maintain that the original concept of a peasant army remains good even in the 1990s.

The self-esteem of the PLA will be hit as internal debate rages on the justice of using the 'people's army' against the people.

Long-term effects are harder to judge but it is certain that officer recruitment will decline from university and college-trained young people. This will also cause a knock-on effect of limiting the modernisation programme because of the lack of highly trained, technology-orientated personnel. The PLA will lose reliable sources of Western military hardware and technology into the early 1990s and will have to bear an increased military budget burden due to the need to increase the research and development sums to counter this loss of Western equipment.

Some developing nations can be expected to re-export military equipment to China but this will lead to increased expenditures in order to purchase this Western hardware.

A Chinese proverb states that "it is better to have no son than one who is a soldier" and this will be borne in mind by many Chinese in the next few years.

The role of the PLA and its use to re-establish centralised order in Beijing will have an effect through the rank structure. The internal suppression role is one not cherished by Defence Minister General Qin Jiwei and his immediate followers. The fact that it was a bloody massacre precipitated by units of the 27th Group Army has also brought PLA and division-level commanders at odds with

The Chinese proverb that states: "It is better to have no son than one who is a soldier" will be borne in mind by many Chinese in the next few years.

each other, which in time will result in major purges within the ranks of China's military, potentially as early as late June.

University educated youth, whom the PLA has been seeking to recruit, have been completely disillusioned as a result of the fighting along the Avenue of Eternal Peace (Changan Avenue). Many opportunities to acquire young, educated officers for the PLA have been squandered and this may take a decade to recover. The PLA will still be able to recruit poorly educated peasant youth from urban areas as conscripts; victims of the economic dislocation that traditionally accompanies economic reforms.

What is occurring now in China is closely akin to the final days of past Chinese dynasties and the effects of the actions in Tiananmen Square are the causes and effects of Chinese factionalism. Western newspapers reported fighting in the outlying districts of Beijing in the week following 3/4 June and often predicted civil war.

Despite the initial concern for civil war in the week following the Tiananmen massacre, China has in most cases resolved its political and politico-military disputes through compromise and the balancing of power. As China analyst William Whitson has noted, "the major factor in the resolution of crucial issues has probably been the determination of regionally based, Party-military leaders to preserve what they consider an appropriate share of power, influence, and prestige for their military system relative to other systems." The PLA has in this case been relied upon to preserve parochial interests.

William Whitson's study, The Chinese High Command (1973) while of greater historical relevance to party-military relationships prior to the 10th Party Congress, has the relevant conclusion: 'party-military personal relations remain a key factor "in reaching compromises on national policy."'

What to many seemed like a developing civil war and challenge to the loyalty of the 27th Group Army to Li Peng by other Group Army-level commanders, has been settled in the interests of maintaining the existing national government in Beijing and Party-control over the military 'bad iron' or no 'bad iron'.

The Future of The People's Liberation Army

The PLA has emerged from the Tiananmen Square crisis in less of a mess than many thought likely. The basics of its power and relationships with the Party remain untouched. The PLA was called in by part of the Party to restore law and order. After some ineffective and then bloody action, order

In the aftermath of the chaos in Tiananmen Square, the PLA will be relying on the support of the civil authorities to say that what they did was right.

was restored and the Army left the streets. To some extent, the fate of the PLA now depends on whether the civilian leadership is able to govern effectively.

The implications of recent events can be divided into a number of categories. First, what does it say about civil-military relations? Most obviously, the old lesson of the Cultural Revolution and 1976 is confirmed; when the Party is divided, the Army is likely to be drawn in to support one side. By and large, the Army will be successful in its task, even though there is some initial uncertainty.

In the June 1989 case, the task was to restore basic law and order. This required clearing the streets and making it clear to the population that there was no point in further demonstrations. Basic level law and order was quickly established. Yet this is far from the end of the story. The other lesson of military intervention is that when the Army enters politics, politics enters the Army. It seems unlikely that the PLA will give up its leading role without there being a clear sense of a firm and credible Party authority able to govern. Given the recent unrest, especially in Beijing, it may take some time for such credibility to be established.

But there looks like being relatively fewer changes in the civilian leadership than first thought (three of 18 Politburo members). If such relative stability is sustained, then the outlook for the PLA must be brighter. The more united the leadership, the more likely the PLA will be able to get back to the professional pursuits to which it has grown used.

The PLA sees improving prospects that, because events have not dragged on as long as during the Cultural Revolution, it will be back to the barracks fairly soon. The new, more professional PLA is clearly more interested in going back to the barracks than the Cultural Revolution version of the armed forces. But the prospects for returning to professional pursuits depends on the changing political order and the ability to pursue economic reform. Without economic reform, the economy will not grow and the PLA will not get the new equipment it was promised before the recent upheaval. What is more, the death of Deng and of some other key figures in the conservation camp might well re-open the entire affair. Predictions are difficult enough, but they are impossible after the point of Deng's death or incapacitation.

If verdicts are reversed after some time, then the attitude towards the PLA may also change. Good civil-military relations require the civil authority

The fate of the Chief of the General Staff, Chi Haotian, was at one time in question. It now seems that Chi has emerged with his reputation intact.

to agree that what the PLA did was correct. Even though it might be shown that the PLA was not uniform in its actions and that it was directed by a specific type of leadership, it will still be true that the PLA followed orders to fire on the people. Thus any major reversal of verdicts on the events of May/June will mean serious problems for the PLA.

The possibility of any reversal of verdicts seems to be declining as it emerges that the civilian leadership was more united than first thought. But if Deng cannot last long enough to allow the new leadership to find its footing, the chance of yet another swing in Chinese policy increases. Failure to pursue economic reform will also mean the chances of the new leaders holding on to power will be reduced.

Second, there is the question of factional struggles in the PLA. Despite all the rumours, the scale of PLA factionalism appears to have been much less than originally suggested. NATO sources suggest that generals below the Group Army level were removed as it became clear that they would not obey orders, but there is no hard evidence as yet about the scale of such resistance. But the clear out was small, and effective enough, that when it came to the time for fighting, there was no significant opposition from the forces on the firing line. There are few reliable bits of evidence of PLA fighting each other intentionally. At the squad level, in the confusion of the early fighting, hundreds of deaths were inflicted by other soldiers. The 1000 or so soldiers killed in this operation (according to NATO sources) involved some death from 'friendly fire' but apparently this was the result of error. Some ordinary soldiers did refuse to carry out orders, but there were not many. Most cases resulted from the uncertainty that followed, such as military incompetence and poor communication which led to the stranding and isolation of convoys.

Most discussion of PLA factionalism hinged on the fact that some military leaders had not been seen until 9 June — almost four days after the events in the Square. The fate of the Defence Minister, General Qin Jiwei and Chief of (the General) Staff, General Chi Haotian were particular focuses of discussion. But it seems that no military official of the first rank has suffered especially as Qin and Chi appeared, along with all members of the Military Affairs Commission except Zhao Ziyang, a civilian Politburo member.

However, it does appear that some generals at the divisional level may have refused orders. The very fact that troops had to be brought in from different regions suggests that not only was the scale of the problem greater than the Beijing Garrison could face, but also that there was some question of the loyalty of certain troops. The Beijing district 38th Group Army was most often mentioned as one with suspect loyalties, or at least suspect resolve when given a difficult order. It remains possible that much of the indecision and failure in military operations had more to do with military incompetence than splits within the PLA. The NATO sources point to the failure in logistics and communications as laying the groundwork for some of the more devastating errors such as the destruction of a convoy of over 100 military vehicles. But in general it appears that the PLA looks like remaining relatively united, especially so long as it can go back to professional pursuits fairly soon. It is possible that the PLA will leave a few of its leaders in more important political positions as guarantors of a stable political environment.

Third, the possibility of a coup or civil war seems less relevant. Civil war was never really on the cards in the true sense. Most of the peasants in the countryside were removed from the events in Beijing and other major cities. Without a mass movement in the countryside, civil war and revolution were impossible.

But there were apparently some differences between regions, although it is too difficult to be sure whether the differences in loyalty were acute or merely aggravating. There has been no case of the PLA in any place other than Beijing being unable to cope with events. Thus we are talking about the risk of a coup d'etat, because the major struggles were taking place at the apex of power in Beijing. But as has become apparent, no significant military leader looks like being purged, thereby refuting the notion of fundamental splits in the armed forces.

Indeed, the formal meaning of the word coup d'etat would require the military taking power for its owns ends against the desire of the civil authority. As has already been explained, recent events can best be described as military intervention at the behest of the dominant civil faction which was unable to establish order on its own. If the moderate forces opposed to martial law had used troop to depose the conservatives, that would have constituted a coup d'etat.

The fourth question about power realignments in the Party and People's Liberation Army can hardly be answered yet. The signs are that the moderate forces such as Party leader Zhao will suffer. But at the time of writing, it is not yet clear whether he will fall as far as Madame Mao (Chiang

Qiao Shi, the party's top internal security officer, looks set to be the new party leader following the removal of Zhao Ziyang.

Ching), Hua Guofeng, or Hu Yaobang. No other Politburo member apart from Hu Qili appears to be in serious trouble, at least for the immediate future.

The rise of Qiao Shi seems clear although it is possible he is part of conservative-leaning compromise. After all, Li Peng might have taken the top Party job. It can be speculated that Li, although apparently surviving, is far from unscathed. His credibility as a leader must be seriously undermined and his fate must be in question. He may hang on until after the death of Deng, or he may go earlier, after a decent interval so as not to show weakness to the moderate forces. There is bound to be a leadership realignment at lower levels in keeping with changes at the top. For example, Hu Qili seems likely to be removed along with Zhao, but the fact that no other Politburo member are under a cloud, suggests the extent of the purge will be something between the scale of the 'post-Gang of Four' operation and the post-Hu

Yaobang case.

Equally, it is reasonable to expect some changes in the military leadership. Even if it is confirmed that no major military leader will be immediately purged, it is possible that some did waver for a time and therefore will be removed in due course. Yang Shangkun seems to have played a pivotal role on the conservative side and therefore should benefit, as long as he stays healthy. But if there was far less division in the PLA than originally surmised, then Yang is not particularly more powerful than he once was. It is reasonable to surmise that military officials at lower levels will rise and fall according to whom they supported.

In sum, the fate of the PLA depends on the fate of the new coalition leaders in charge of China as a whole. Its appears increasingly likely that both China and the PLA will be less deeply scarred by the events of May/June 1989 than first thought. But at least until the succession to Deng Xiaoping is concluded, all bets must be hedged.

Soviet-Chinese Relations — A Historical Perception

The reverence accorded by the official Chinese media since the early 1970s to Genghis Khan, the thirteenth century Mongol conqueror and ruler of vast territories between the Yellow Sea in the east and the Black Sea in the west, is a stark reminder of the importance of Moscow's relationship with Beijing. The most significant legacy of the centuries of Mongol rule in the thirteenth and fourteenth centuries over what is now the Soviet Union was the moulding of the Russian character and national attitudes.

In the Sino-Soviet dispute of the 1970s the Chinese used the memory of Genghis Khan as an anti-Soviet bogeyman, illustrating how deeply historical the conflict was.

The decline of the Mongol empire under Genghis Khan's successors, and its final break-up, coincided with the rise of a Russian national state under the Grand Dukes of Moscow in the fifteenth and sixteenth centuries. During the second half of the sixteenth century Moscow's rule had penetrated the Urals and spread into Siberia. The process of colonisation eastwards was not the work of regular forces, but was the work of adventurers, traders and merchants escaping the control of the central government. By the 1630s Russian settlers had reached the shores of the Pacific Ocean. Finally, in 1689 the Treaty of Nerchinsk, the first solemn diplomatic agreement between Moscow and Beijing, fixed the frontier between the two empires along the middle course of the Amur River. During the eighteenth century and into the early nineteenth, with Russia's main interest being centred on Western Europe, activity in the Far East was confined mainly to exploration and consolidating the work of settlement begun in the previous century. Early in the reign of Peter the Great

(1689-1725) the Russians established themselves in Kamchatka, followed by expeditions to the Kurile Islands and the coast of the Sea of Okhotsk. In the 1730s Vitus Behring, a Dane in Russian service, travelled widely in the North Pacific and subsequently gave his name to the straits separating Asia from North America. Although Russian attempts to penetrate Japan came to nought, in the late eighteenth century Russian settlements were established on the North American continent, and a United American Company established, which was renamed the Russian-American Company in 1799. Thus, by the end of the century Russia had become a Pacific power.

For almost fifty years Russia's efforts in the Far East were mainly concentrated on attempting to develop relations with Japan, with varying success. In the early 1840s, however, affairs in the Far East took a dramatic new turn. In 1843, Rear Admiral Putyatin proposed to Czar Nicholas I that advantage should be taken of China's defeat by the western powers in the Opium War of 1839-42, and an expedition be sent to explore the mouth of the Amur river to define Russia's frontier with China on the Pacific. Nothing further came of the idea until 1849 when Captain Nevelskoi entered the mouth of the Amur. In 1850 a Russian settlement was established at the mouth of the river, the Czar giving his consent on the ground that "where once the Russian flag has flown, it must not be lowered again". By the mid-1850s Russian policy was shaped as much by the desire not to be left out of the 'scramble for China' as by any hope of profit from commercial ventures. Russian policy was not to be deflected by the Crimean War (1854-56), determined to secure Chinese recognition of the Russian seizure of the mouth of the Amur. The

Russian Government had the opportunity to extract concessions when China once again found itself at war with the Western power in 1856. The Treaty of Tientsin of June 1858 guaranteed the right of Russian subjects to trade with China by sea and land, but left open the sensitive issue of the Russo-Chinese frontier. The technique used to force the Chinese to submit was a mixture of verbal persuasion — with Russian presence on the Amur needed to deter the aggressive British, and the threat of physical force — the deployment of artillery to lend support to diplomacy. In the end the Chinese ceded the left bank of the Amur from its junction with the Argun to the sea to the Russians. The future of the territory between the Ussuri, the Amur and the Pacific was left to further negotiation. The outbreak in 1859 once more of war between China and the Western powers gave the Russians the opportunity to force the pace of negotiations, accompanied by further exploration of the Amur during which the site for a suitable Russian port was chosen further down the coast: the future Vladivostock (Ruler of the East). It is doubtful whether the Chinese would have acceded to Russian demands for all the territory between the Ussuri and the Pacific if the senior Russian negotiator, Count N P Ignat'ev, had not used his influence to prevent the Western powers from sacking Beijing. Negotiations for Russo-Chinese frontier proceeded in a friendlier spirit, and in November 1860 the Treaty of Peking (Beijing) was ratified. Russia received virtually all the territory she had claimed between Ussuri and the Pacific. The building of Vladivostock could now press ahead. Russia's position as a great power in the Northern Pacific was assured.

Russian acquisition of Chinese territory, while posing as the friend of China during the conflict with the Western Powers, was followed later in the century by her support of China in the face of Japanese encroachment on Chinese territory. Following the Japanese abandonment in 1895 of the Liaotung Peninsula, Russia exploited her advantage, securing the Chinese a loan, and in 1896 concluding a treaty of alliance. Under the terms of the treaty Russia was committed to defend China against Japan. Russia could not defend China, however, against the results of her own folly. In 1897, following the murder of two German missionaries by the Chinese, the German Government occupied Kiaochow. This action provided the excuse for the seizure of Chinese territory by other European powers. It was Russia, nonetheless, who took the richest spoil. By a Treaty in March 1898 the Chinese Government ceded the Liaotung Peninsula and Port Arthur to Russia for 25 years.

The acquisition of Liaotung in the long run was to prove fatal for the Russian position in the Far East. She had taken from China without a war what had previously been denied Japan as the fruit of victory in a war. As a demonstration of Russian assertiveness in the Far East, and a threat to fundamental Japanese interests, it was one of the prime elements, driving Russia and Japan into war.

Sino-Soviet Relations — Modern Assessment

After the catastrophes of the Russo-Japanese War (1904-06) it may have seemed that Russia's position in the Far East was doomed. In the period immediately preceding the 1914-1918 War, however, Russia made an astonishing retrieval of the position and power in the region. In the main this was accomplished by *rapprochement* with Japan, and a joint policy of carving up portions of China, now in the last death throws of a 3000 year Imperial history. While Japan took northern Manchuria and tightened her control over Korea, Russia was granted reluctant recognition of her primacy in Outer Mongolia. Although defeat put an end to any expansionist ideas, Russia remained a great power in the Far East.

With regard to relations with China, the pre-1914 policy of carving up China in effect meant that Russia was now 'gamekeeper turned poacher', while the territorial division of the spoils predetermined Russian/Soviet policy in the region well into the last decades of the twentieth century.

Meanwhile war and Revolution in 1917 left Russia especially weak and exposed in the Far East. The initiative lay with Japan, who in co-ordination with China mounted a series of operations into Siberia.

In the wake of the Civil War (1919-22) Soviet policy towards China operated through three agencies: the first — the diplomatic apparatus — sought normalisation of relations; the second, under the nominal control of the Comintern, was interested in the long term revolutionary possibilities inherent in China under Sun Yat-sen; the third, the middle man, was the Red Army command. The latter was a new element in Sino-Soviet relations, destined to play a greater role in the future. For the next 30 years, however, it was the dominant personality of Stalin which was to shape the tortuous course of Sino-Soviet relations.

Until 1946 Stalin pursued a policy of alliance with the Guomindang controlled since 1925 by Chiang Kai-Shek. The partnership survived the massacre in 1927 of the Chinese Communist Party, and ignored the internecine struggles which went on despite the Japanese invasion. Meanwhile, the Chinese Communist Party had survived, and following the 'Long March' of 1934-36 regrouped. Not for the first time, Stalin had misjudged or misread the signs.

From 1943 onwards the Soviet media approach to Chinese affairs began to demonstrate a marked pro-Communist and anti-Nationalist (Guomindang) bias. It was, however, some time before Moscow was to change sides, well aware of the advantage of dealing with the Nationalists while ignoring the Communists. In the long term, however, Stalin appeared to have consistently underestimated and miscalculated the strength of Chinese Communists under the leadership of Mao Zedong. As regards the future of the revolution in China, as one leading Yugoslav Party leader stated in 1948: "They (the Chinese People's Army) are beating the Chiang Kai-Shek army.... It proved that the Chinese comrades and not the Soviet comrades were right."

In January 1949 Beijing fell to the People's Liberation Army, and by the summer practically the whole of the Chinese mainland was under the control of the Communists. The Soviet Union was the first to recognise the formidable addition to the Communist camp, and Mao Zedong was invited to a lengthy and much publicised conference in Moscow, lasting from December 1949 to February 1950. At the close of the conference a Sino-Soviet Treaty was signed, comprising territorial concessions, a military alliance, and a credit of 300 million dollars (equivalent). The Treaty was followed by a series of trade and economic agreements under which China was to supply the Soviet Union with raw materials, in exchange for arms, machinery, and the assistance of Soviet technicians and advisors. The subsequent outbreak of the Korean War in June 1950, and the involvement of China in a military campaign in the interests of a policy stage managed by Moscow appeared to cement the alliance. There were, however, deep rooted problems threatening the long-term Sino-Soviet relationship. As long as Stalin lived and in the immediate aftermath of his death relations were characterised by an identity of interests and long-term objectives.

There was every reason to believe that the Sino-Soviet alliance would be solid and lasting. Each side had much to gain from the partnership, and everything to lose were it to be dissolved. In the first five years Soviet loans to china totalled US$1.3 million. The Soviet Union had backed China during the Korean War, including the despatch of a high-level group of military advisors. Later there was Soviet support over China's claim to Taiwan, and her demand for a seat on the Security Council. In the first years of Communist rule, Soviet scientific collaboration and a training programme for thousands of students at Soviet universities were vital assets to the growing China. Finally, Soviet military aid to the People's Liberation Army was considerable. In return, Beijing was prepared to acknowledge Soviet leadership of the Communist Bloc, and to support Soviet policy, including the suppression of the Hungarian uprising in 1956 and on the question of Germany's future.

While there was no question of China becoming a member of the Warsaw Pact, a Chinese observer was present at the signing in May 1955, and China expressed support for its aims. Even over the prickly issue of ideology the Chinese generally accepted Soviet pronouncements, while at times attempting to produce a Chinese interpretation of the point in question. In short, to the world at large the impression was of a solid united Communist front in which Moscow was the acknowledged leader.

Beneath the surface, however, the Chinese, conscious of the long-standing contribution to the evolution of world Communism, believed they were entitled to experiment their own in home and foreign affairs, and could detect no reason why the Soviet Union should object. There were, nonetheless, Chinese innovations affecting claims to authority in the Communist world which Moscow could not renounce without seriously weakening her position of supremacy. By the late 1950s criticism was being expressed, on both sides, of certain policies and trends. The Soviet Union, for example, did not believe that Chinese views expressed in Mao Zedong's liberation campaign 'Let a hundred flowers bloom, let a hundred schools of thought contend' were applicable to the Soviet Union. The Chinese for their part attributed error in the Five Year Plan to officials basing themselves on the 'Soviet experience'. Despite these first signs of dissention, the gathering of the world communist parties in Moscow in November 1957 to celebrate the 40th anniversary of the October Revolution was an opportunity for the Chinese to proclaim loyalty to the Soviet leadership, now in the hands of Nikita Khrushchev.

Despite acknowledging Soviet ideological and political leadership in November 1957, within a year the Chinese were to launch an economic and social revolution, claiming to speed up the pace of evolution towards Communism: the Commune. The 'great leap forward' was announced by the Chinese leadership in May 1958. The experiment failed, and the Soviet leadership, in an attempt to limit the damage to the alliance, showed a willingness to ease the Chinese party out of turmoil of its own making. The Soviet grip on military,

scientific, and industrial aid to China was probably still a significant factor in both Soviet and Chinese calculations. The underlying ideological dispute was soon to be sharpened by events affecting the Soviet Union's relations with other world powers, notably the United States and India. During the Sino-Indian border disputes throughout 1959 and 1960 Moscow attempted to adopt an impartial attitude, showing understanding for the Chinese case in public, while at the same time stressing close Soviet ties with India. A new element of disagreement arose over Soviet attempts to achieve *rapprochement* with the United States. This move stemmed from the Soviet attitude to war and peace, and when visiting Beijing in October 1959, Khrushchev warned China not to place too much confidence in war to achieve political objectives.

The 90th anniversary of Lenin's birth in April 1960 was the opportunity for the Chinese leadership to declare that 'war' is an inevitable outcome of the exploiting system. The same year the Soviet Union withdrew all Soviet advisors from China. By 1961 the Sino-Soviet rift was at its worst, demonstrated by Khrushchev's open attack on Albania, China's satellite, at the 22nd Party Congress. In the years that followed the split, the momentous rift between the two became apparent for all to see. The dispute between Moscow and Beijing came into the open, couched at first in ideological verbage regarding 'co-existence', 'revisionism', 'dogmatism', 'cult of personality'. Before long it descended into verbal abuse, suggesting a deeper personal antipathy between Khrushchev and Mao Zedong.

What was at stake, however, was the contest for the leadership of the world revolutionary movement, with the split between Moscow and Beijing in turn exercising momentous repercussions in communist parties throughout the world. Khrushchev's successors fared little better in dealing with Mao Zedong. After a brief attempt at reconciliation and reticence in public Brezhnev was to find himself engaged in polemics and hostility equally as bitter as in Khrushchev's time.

What was to inject a fundamentally new

dimension into the Sino-Soviet rift was the gradual build-up of Soviet forces along the border with China. In the late 1960s and early 1970s the Soviet Union was deploying strategic missiles in the Transbaikal and Siberian Military Districts. Following the clashes between Soviet and Chinese border troops on Damansky Island in 1969 the Soviet High Command stepped-up its military effectiveness, reaching around 400 000 men in almost 50 divisions. While probably over half this total were ground forces, there was also a significant increase in the air forces, with over 2000 combat aircraft far superior in performance than anything the Chinese possessed. The Soviet Pacific Fleet based at Vladivostock was considerably expanded, with almost 800 vessels by 1979. Of this total some 70 were major surface vessels and 80 submarines. In addition naval infantry strength was brought up to around 5000 men. Naval aviation, with some 300 aircraft with support equipment, providing a third major strike force.

At the same time, the Soviet Union attempted to develop the economic resources of the region, constructing a new strategic railway, the Baikal-Amur Line (BAM), running parallel some 200-500 km north of the Trans-Siberian Railway.

The signature of the Sino-Vietnam Agreement in 1978, and the Soviet invasion of Afghanistan in December 1979 greatly increased Sino-Soviet tension. The Soviet-Vietnam Agreement was followed in February 1979 by a Chinese attack on Vietnam herself. This move coincided with the creation of the Soviet Far East Forces Command in late 1978, comprising the Transbaikal, Far East and Siberian Military Districts, under the command of Army General V I Petrov.

The speech in Tashkent by Brezhnev in 1979 was probably the first attempt in public by a Soviet leader to defuse the situation. It fell on stony ground and was finally buried by the Soviet invasion of Afghanistan. The move on the part of the Soviet leadership to attempt a *rapprochement* was not to be repeated until 1986, when in a speech at Vladivostock the new Soviet leader, Mikhail Gorbachev, for the first time appeared to make moves to appease the Chinese leadership: partial

withdrawal of Soviet troops from Outer Mongolia; withdrawal from Afghanistan; and the declaration of the Pacific 'dream' of peace following significant Soviet forces reductions in the Far East.

To be sure, Gorbachev was in fact building on foundations that had already been laid in the early 1980s. Sino-Soviet consultations had been in progress since 1981. By 1983 when the third round was held in Beijing, while no breakthrough appeared to have been achieved on major issues, there was limited progress in matters of economic exchange, and local agreements. A further round of talks in Moscow the same year produced further limited progress on border trading points. At the same time Chinese and Soviet officials were making gestures to improve the atmosphere, such as attendance at National Day celebration. There was also a sign of slackening of harsh attitudes towards Beijing on the part of the Soviet Union Eastern bloc allies. Neither side, however, appeared entirely willing to drop its public polemics against each other. Nonetheless, as the Chinese press was to point out in 1986, several 'milestones in Sino-Soviet relations' had been achieved: the holding of a large trade fair in Moscow in July, the first for almost 30 years; the significant expansion in local trade contracts; the establishment of consulates in Shangai and Leningrad; the dispatch of several hundred Soviet experts to help China modernise factory equipment, in some cases set up by the Soviet Union under the 1950s aid programme. In 1987 the Soviet Union sent a high-level construction delegation to China to work out a programme for capital construction projects.

It was, however, on the crucial issues, and Soviet moves to accommodate Chinese demands, that were to be the test of Soviet good faith. These included the significant reduction of nuclear weapons (SS20s); substantial reductions of conventional forces in the border region; the withdrawal from Afghanistan; and, Soviet pressure on Vietnam to withdraw from Cambodia. Significant Soviet concessions in all these areas opened the way to the visit of the Soviet leader to Beijing 15-18 May 1989.

In the Soviet press the visit was hailed as ending

'the thirty-year old chill', marking the normalisation 'of the strained relations between the world's biggest and most populous countries'. The communiqué issued at the end of the visit, in the Soviet view 'puts relations between the two socialist countries on the stable basis of respect for each other's sovereignty and territorial integrity, non-aggression, non-interference, equality, mutual benefit and peaceful co-existence'. Both sides expressed their determination to solve all contentious issues between them 'by way of peaceful talks'. Agreement was also reached to reduce each country's armed forces in the area of the Sino-Soviet border. Talks were to be stepped up on outstanding border issues.

There is no doubt that Gorbachev's mission to Beijing is a milestone in the post war Sino-Soviet relationship, despite the ominous and embarrassing background of student unrest which caused the Gorbachev welcome to be re-scheduled. That relationship traditionally has rested on two fundamental elements: a shared border and common ideological roots. Fundamental differences in both spheres have brought the two nations to the brink of war in the past. While the Soviet Union has undoubtedly made substantial concessions to the Chinese, the final resolution of the border dispute could test will on both sides. Imperial Russian acquisition of large areas of the former Chinese Empire in the nineteenth century was the foundation of her claim to be a Pacific power. The return of these territories would mark the end of a Soviet claim to a predominant role in the Pacific, a claim the Chinese have never been willing to accept. Many Chinese are deeply sceptical that the Soviets will ever deliver on their new promises.

China's Southern Neighbours

'Nations do not have perpetual allies,
just perpetual interests'

Chinese involvement in South East Asia falls perfectly in line with this age-old principle. Chinese 'foreign policy' has always been to maintain a ring of tributary states or friendly countries around it as a buffer zone against unwelcome foreign intervention. These states would not necessarily recognise formal Chinese sovereignty but would bear Chinese interests and Chinese opinion closely to mind when deciding upon their actions. Where possible Chinese contact with outsiders would be maintained only within the ring of allied states. Trading and other 'friendly' contacts could take place there as easily as anywhere else. Unavoidable hostilities would be fought, if possible, using the armed forces of the friendly powers. Only as a last resort would China mobilise its own forces to

China has been quick to use its military might to quell internal disturbance and to secure its annexations of neighbouring nations, like Tibet. In 1988, the PLA formed a quick reaction force, the 15th Airborne Division for such a role.

engage in conflict outside its borders.

An important factor in Chinese foreign policy is a deeply-implanted fear of contact with the outside world and of the disruption and contamination caused by 'outside' ideas. If such ideas seem to be disrupting the political and social order of Chinese society they will have to be suppressed with the utmost vigour. The current purge of 'activist' students and members of the intelligentsia following the Tiananmen Square pro-democracy demonstrations and subsequent massacre is a good example of this suppression. The fact that some students are being surrendered to the authorities by members of their own families bears witness to the speed and effectiveness of state control.

China's recent assertion of sovereignty over Tibet and the violent suppression of the dissident movement there is another example of this trend. That country is viewed as part of China's innermost defence perimeter and one that therefore receives the strictest controls. Attempts by the Tibetans to loosen those controls will always be put down promptly and with great violence. The PLA has also been instrumental in the establishment of Chinese ethnic groups in the Tibetan region and has protected them against the actions of local guerilla movements which have been operating on an opportunity basis since 1959. China always sees the hand of India in all modern events in Tibet.

India and China have been engaged in border skirmishes which have led to all-out border war on at least one occasion. In 1962, China annexed the Ashai Chin pass and continued to press for control

Chinese forces suffered greater losses than they needed to during the Vietnamese campaign because of the lack of field ambulances and casualty evacuation. Part of the modernisation programme has seen the development of the armoured machine.

of several other high Himalayan access routes. Since then, using Pakistan as a surrogate, China has continued to apply pressure on India. China actively supports Pakistan with military equipment and diplomatic leverage in the latter's battle for control of Kashmir.

Burma, falls to a lesser extent into China's foreign policy ambit. Hardly worth considering as a potential ally, China nonetheless fosters various factions within the country in order to retain a 'vote' in the event of the whole ramshackle edifice collapsing.

Chinese action taken in Korea during 1950-53, Indo-China during the 1960s and the Sino-Vietnamese conflict of February/March 1979 falls neatly into its traditional foreign policy pattern.

In Korea the US presence in the southern part of the country was seen as a potential threat to be contained by the Chinese satellite state in the North. The destruction of this satellite by US military power and the advance of US forces to within a few kilometres of the Chinese border brought about a direct Chinese military participation. Once the situation was stabilised the Chinese returned home.

In Vietnam the increasing US involvement was again seen as a threat to China's security perimeter and was initially resisted using support for the North Vietnamese and Vietcong forces. In this case, the US was defeated by those Vietnamese forces making a Chinese entry unnecessary.

Vietnam has always been an anomalous part of China's world view. Although undoubtedly a part of the Chinese defence perimeter, it has historically

The PLA Navy has a formidable surface-to-surface missile capability which could be an important factor in any conflict over disputed territorial waters.

been a recalcitrant, unwilling and sometimes hostile part of the system. Numerous Chinese armies have come to grief in the Indo-Chinese peninsular and the Chinese themselves have rarely won the acceptance which they have found in nearby countries. It was not surprising that relations between China and Vietnam soured so quickly after the US withdrawal, indeed it was more a case of reverting to type.

Although Chinese policy appears to have made a dramatic switch in the 1970s, from supporting the communist forces of North Vietnam to backing the west-leaning forces of Thailand, this is not the case. Chinese perceptions were shaped by the massive Soviet support for the Vietnamese government and the growing influence of Soviet policy makers within that country. To the Chinese this was the ultimate nightmare — their own policy of a chain of border allies fighting incursions into China by proxy being turned against them. A new ally was needed to fight the intruder — now the Soviet Union, not the USA.

China's tradition of short, sharp punishments meted out to uncooperative client states failed disastrously when tried against Vietnam in 1979. The Vietnamese units, well dug in and lavishly supported, inflicted heavy casualties on the 33 divisions of advancing Chinese infantry. Despite being outnumbered and giving ground for time, the Vietnamese forces were able to respond well, especially after both Hanoi and Haiphong were threatened.

Outside sources say that Chinese co-ordination and military discipline broke down under the onslaught of a Vietnamese counter-offensive but Chinese sources have always maintained that the PLA withdrew in good order. The Chinese had intended to wear down the Vietnamese units, forcing them to expend their manpower in a defensive battle. Instead it was the Chinese units which suffered the attrition and eventually it became obvious that the engagement could not be sustained. The Vietnamese Army had won what in retrospect seems certain was its last victory on land but pressure continues over the Spratley Islands and other territorial water disputes. The relationship between Vietnam and China is dormant at best.

China's relations with her important neighbour southern Thailand have been complex. China has been a supporter of the displaced Khmer Rouge forces, now sheltering in refugee camps along the Thai/Cambodian border after the overthrow of the Pol Pot dictatorship in December 1978.

If the guerilla forces, numbering about 25 000, were to engage the Vietnamese Army on China's behalf with any hope of success they have to receive large supplies of military equipment quickly. This could only come by way of Thailand and with the co-operation of the Thai government. Thailand was also the last stable, independent but reasonably powerful country left in Indo-China. At this time the Communist insurgency in Thailand was collapsing at the hands of a well-conceived and skilfully executed counter-insurgency campaign. There was no prospect of the existing government in Thailand being replaced by one of Chinese choice so the only option left was to befriend the one already there. It was also apparent that the Royal Thai Army was incapable of acting as a counterbalance to the massive and well trained Vietnamese forces which numbered about 180 000 men and women in the mid 1980s.

This left the Chinese with few options. Friendly relations with Thailand had to be instituted if support for existing Chinese allies in the area was to continue. Thailand had already adopted a hawkish role in the area, based on its fears of a direct Vietnamese attack on Thai territory. Such an attack could be launched from Vietnamese bases in Cambodia, barely 60 km from Bangkok. China instituted a policy of diplomatic support for

Thailand has maintained a working relationship with China and continues to show an interest in obtaining Chinese hardware. China in turn sees Thai as a stable neighbour and has offered equipment on 'friendship' terms.

the Thai position on Indo-China, demanding an immediate Vietnamese pull-out from Kampuchea and Laos. By the middle of the 1980s this relationship took a step further when China commenced deliveries of military equipment to the Royal Thai Army.

For Thailand the Chinese support was welcome on a number of grounds. In addition to the obvious added security provided and the valuable political points gained from the contacts with China, the growing relationship provided Thailand with additional negotiating strength in dealing with its ASEAN (Association of South East Asian Nations) partners. The country has always been uneasy about its dependence on US military hardware and the offer of supplies from China was irresistible on political as well as military and economic grounds. Although most Thai officers regard the quality of Chinese armaments with derision, the fact remains they break the pattern of dependence upon a single source.

At the beginning of 1989 Thailand had ordered more than a hundred Type 69 tanks, over eight hundred YWH-532 armoured personnel carriers and small quantities of artillery pieces from China. The Royal Thai Navy had previously ordered four frigates from Chinese shipyards with discussions being started on a fifth to act as a training ship. The Royal Thai Air Force would soon be evaluating the F-7M Airguard (upgraded Soviet-designed MiG-21) fighter to meet at least some of its requirements. In order to ensure an adequate flow of support for the new equipment, a stockpile of spares and ammunition was to be established in Thailand.

The Thai perception of the recent unrest in China is that, first and foremost it is China's internal affair and should not affect her external relations. Sources in Thailand have pointed out that although the trouble in China was far more widespread than was realised at the time, it also subsided far quicker than western observers had believed it would. Such eruptions of popular feeling happen at regular intervals of about every 20 years in China. Some concern was expressed that the Vietnamese withdrawal from Cambodia might be delayed by China's internal pre-occupations. Informed sources inside the Thai Army correctly predicted a period of purging, mostly of middle level government members and of civilian dissenters. Current policy in Thailand will undoubtedly be to put a hold on agreements with China for a couple of months until the situation has cooled down. The order for F-7M Airguard fighters should be confirmed at the end of the period.

With Vietnam in economic collapse and 'retreating' towards its own borders, the Chinese need for a Thai alliance has faded, making the prospects of a longer term relationship more questionable. The exceptionally low 'friendship prices' being charged by the Chinese for their military hardware are already fading and there has been a rapid escalation of ammunition and spares costs.

The F-7 Airguard combat aircraft is developed from the Soviet-built MiG-21. These are early versions seen in Chinese service and without the benefit of Western technology. Export of that technology is now doubtful after the events in Tiananmen Square.

China's Eastern Neighbour

China and Japan normalised bilateral relations in 1972 after nearly three decades of hostilities, occupation and scorn. Both nations saw the economic realities of normalising day-to-day affairs and the first Sino-Japanese Friendship Treaty was signed in 1978.

Although there had been signs that China and Japan had buried a hatchet first wielded centuries before, the recent re-writing of Japanese school history books and the continued build-up of the Japanese armed forces have continued to strain the relationship. China is suspicious of Japan, always has been and probably always will be so.

China is very aware of Japanese economic power and its people do not need a long memory to remember the impact of Imperial Japanese military power. The fact that Japan feels vulnerable to Soviet power and hosts considerable US military power, including nuclear-capable strike aircraft and long-range maritime patrol aircraft on its soil, does not go unnoticed either.

Yet China has been active in trying to encourage

China's vast army with good armoured support continues to concern Japan as much as the recent build-up of the Japanese Self-Defence Force offends the Chinese. Japan and China both need the security of a mutually ratified Treaty of Friendship.

Japanese high technology industry to co-operate with its own domestic military modernisation. Computer technology is especially important to China and it is possible that the Japanese have made available the Chinese character computer – five-stroke input- technology developed by Wang Yongming – to the Chinese military as reported in *Jane's Defence Weekly*, 1 October 1988.

Until Tiananmen Square, the future of Sino-Japanese relations had been expected to depend on the Deng-Gorbachev Summit and the opening of trade barriers across the Sino-Soviet frontiers. The United States government even then was concerned about making more and more high technology available to China, especially through Japan. The Toshiba allegations about high technology transfers to the Soviet Union and China remain prominent in the minds of both Houses of Congress.

Both Japan and the USA have been concerned about the Chinese success in exporting weaponry and military technology to nations engaged in conflict. During the Gulf conflict, Japanese and US merchant ships came under attack from Iranian forces with a variety of weapons, including the HY-2 'Silkworm' surface-to-surface guided missile. China became, in mid 1988, the largest arms supplier to the belligerent parties.

The PLA and the Drive for Modernisation

"The PLA—the Great Wall of steel, safeguarding the security and socialist construction of our motherland

"The recent student unrest is not going to lead to any major disturbances. But because of its nature it must be taken very seriously. Firm measures must be taken against any student who creates trouble in Tiananmen Square. The rules and regulations on marches and demonstrations *promulgated by the Standing Committee of the Municipal People's Congress of Beijing have the force of law and should be resolutely enforced. No concession should be made in this matter. In the beginning, we mainly used persuasion, which is as it should be in dealing with student demonstrators. But if any of them disturb public order or violate the law, they must be dealt with unhesitatingly. Persuasion includes application of the law. When*

Deng Xiapong deals 'unhesitatingly' with those who disturb public order. Beijing residents hide behind cars as troop trucks drive by on 7 June. Soldiers in similar vehicles fired indiscriminately as they passed.

a disturbance breaks out in a place, it's because the leaders there did not take a firm clear-cut stand. This is not a problem that has arisen in just one or two places or in just the last couple of years; it is the result of failure over the past several years to take a firm, clear-cut stand against bourgeois liberalisation. It is essential to adhere firmly to the Four Cardinal Principles; otherwise bourgeois liberalisation will spread unchecked — and that has been the root cause of the problem. but this student unrest is also a good thing insofar as it is a reminder to us...

"There is no way to ensure continued political stability and unity without the people's dictatorship. People who confuse right and wrong, who turn black into white, who start rumours and spread slanders can't be allowed to go around with impunity stirring the masses up to make trouble. A few years ago we punished according to the law some exponents of liberalisation who broke the law. Did that bring discredit on us? No, China's image was not damaged. On the contrary, the prestige of our country is steadily growing."
(Deng Xiaoping 30 December 1986)

These words of Deng were uttered in a speech to leading members of the Central Committee of the Chinese Communist Party in *1986*, not 1989. Accurate and prophetic in its hint of what would happen to demonstrating students in 1989, this speech proved to be grossly inaccurate in its assessment of the international reaction to the People's Liberation Army's brutal suppression of the student demonstrators in Tiananmen Square.

The savagery of the PLA's assault on unarmed civilians, in full view of the international news media, has provoked near universal condemnation of the Chinese Communist Party and the People's Liberation Army. It has resulted in a drastic setback to the Chinese military modernisation programme by the cancellation of Western military equipment

Tiananmen Square provides the venue for regular military parades in Beijing. Onlookers at this parade would never have thought that the military hardware (130 mm self-propelled howitzers) so proudly displayed could have been turned against them.

and technology exports to China.

Why did the Communist Party leadership act in the way it did? Why did it misjudge the international reaction to its Tiananmen massacre so badly?

The answers to these questions can be looked for in the history and ideology of the Communist Party of China and of the dual functions — political and military — of its own armed force the People's Liberation Army; in the personal experiences of the Chinese leadership; and in the nature of life in China today.

Of all national armed forces in the twentieth century, China's communist armies have had perhaps the hardest history over a protracted period of time. Since their birth in the 1920s the Communist armed forces have had several names,

By 1953, the Chinese PLA had developed from its peasant roots into the beginnings of an integrated force. The predominance of artillery began in the 1950s and by the late 1980s there was more soldiers 'cap-badged' gunners than infantry.

Militiawomen from South China demonstrate their marksmanship. Mao Zedong believed in a 'Red' Army rather than a high technology-based force. He encouraged the use of peasant militias.

beginning as the First Workers' and Peasants Red Army, later being named the Red Army – with Route Armies – and finally in July 1946 grouped together under the collective title of the People's Liberation Army. They have survived a tough military test of fire: decades of civil war against the Guomindang (a war which is technically still not over as long as Taiwan exists in its present state — in the early years, these conflicts nearly led to extermination of the embryo PLA) war against the Japanese; and war against the United States and other United Nations forces in the Korean War. After the proclamation of the People's Republic in 1949, the PLA was occupied with invasion and suppression campaigns in Tibet and border clashes with Taiwan, India, the Soviet Union and Vietnam. The PLA is a hard army in a harsh environment. It has not had an opportunity to go soft.

The PLA is the national army of the People's Republic of China, but it has another role — as the army of the Chinese Communist Party, for which it has had internal security and political functions to fulfil, acting to suppress uprisings and dissent within China and within the Communist Party itself. The June 1989 Tiananmen action by the

Modernisation for the PLA includes the development of military vehicles. These Type 69-II main battle tanks are a development of a Chinese copy of a Soviet design. Export versions include European and North American sub-systems, including fire control systems and main guns.

The Chinese aviation industry has been busy developing copies of Soviet aircraft and fitting Western equipment to make them more saleable to Third World countries.

PLA is only the most recent in a series of internal suppression campaigns carried out by the Army. It has, however, been the most widely publicised and spectacular; in the past the world's media were not watching, or waiting for the historic arrival of a charismatic Soviet political leader. Mikhail Gorbachev.

The history of Chinese Communism has seen a series of intense personality and faction clashes within the Communist Party, with control of the PLA sometimes being the crucial factor in deciding the winner in these clashes. The PLA has at various times in its short life been torn between the desire to develop as a modern professional military force capable of fighting an all-arms conventional war, and its commitment as a Party political force for the propagation of ideology and the elimination or suppression of opponents and dissidents. In Tiananmen Square in June the latter role came to the fore.

The early Communist Party army established in 1927 had as its first priorities survival and the creation of a disciplined force with adequate levels of equipment and training from minimal resources This rural-based army arose out of the failure of the Soviet Comintern-directed policy of Communist Party co-operation with Chiang Kai-shek's Guomindang, and attempting an urban uprising.

When this collaboration broke down.

Modernisation for China includes the development of the nuclear industry and other very advanced technology programmes. This is China's first tandem particle accelerator.

Chinese engineers and technicians have developed their own anti-aircraft missile defence systems such as this unnamed type displayed in 1988. (Jane's Defence Weekly)

Guomindang forces massacred large numbers of Communist supporters. From this time on the Communist Party and its poorly equipped and untrained small new armies were forced to become almost entirely self-reliant — ideologically, materially and doctrinally. This sense of self-reliance was to be portrayed for many years as a virtue (albeit made out of a necessity) until disastrous losses in modern conventional warfare in Korea forced the PLA to implement a crash modernisation programme during the war and in the years following its close.

From 1927 until 1937 the Red Armies were on the defensive, with survival and the development of a strategy for success in the future being the main priorities. It was during this period that Mao Zedong formulated his theories of rural guerilla warfare with popular support — People's War — which have had such a pervasive influence on Chinese Communist military thinking and the thinking of other Communist movements throughout the world. The failure of further attempts at urban warfare in 1930 confirmed the wisdom of following a strategy of limited military goals attempted with limited military resources. Military campaigns were mounted, but these were often designed to help build up Communist forces — recruiting defectors, capturing weapons, ammunition and equipment, securing base areas and spreading propaganda. A number of Chinese Communist soldiers returned from the Soviet Union where they had received advanced training. Along with some of the outstanding Red Army leaders, such as Peng Dehuai, these officers helped to establish a curriculum for the Red Army academy at Juichin, and helped establish tactical doctrine using Soviet manuals.

The Guomindang forces were stronger than the Red Armies, and were able to profit from the advice of German military advisors under General Hans von Seeckt, the recently retired Chief of the German General Staff. By 1934 the Guomindang forces, in their Fifth Encirclement Campaign, were seriously threatening the Kiangsi Soviet base area, and Communist survival. The momentous decision was taken to leave this area and seek a safer base area further north. The First Front Army under Zhu De and Mao Zedong, along with the Second Front Army and the Fourth Front Army, broke out of their encircled bases and set out on a journey, the Long March, of 11 100 kilometres through hostile and inhospitable territory, pursued and attacked at various times by the Guomindang. Zhu De's First Front Army, in which Mao Zedong was political commissar, covered the distance in thirteen months. According to one source 'this was the longest and fastest sustained march ever made under combat conditions by any army of foot troops, and has been exceeded in rate of march over a long distance only by a few Mongol expeditions of the 13th Century'.

Casualties and non combat losses on the Long March were very high, possibly as high as 90 per cent of the original 90-100 000 who began the March. But the nucleus of the Red Army was preserved and 'the core of its participants formed a cohesive leadership that remained largely intact for three decades'. According to Mao, 'if his men could survive that they could survive anything'. An indication of the primitive state of the Red Army's equipment at this time can be gauged from the displays of simple, hand-made equipment proudly displayed in the large Long March section of the Military Museum of the Chinese People's Revolution in Beijing.

In post -1949 China, participation in the Long March confers great status and influence on its survivors — membership of an elite — and Long March veterans have dominated the Communist Party and the PLA. They, no doubt, believe that they fully deserve the eternal respect and obedience of the rest of the Party and country. They also appear to make the greatest claims to ideological correctness. Deng Xiaoping is a survivor of the

Long March, and his views remain resolutely opposed to political liberalisation, as the following extracts from a 1986 speech indicate:

"With regard to the question of opposing bourgeois liberalisation, I am the one who has talked about it most often and most insistently. Why? First, because there is now a trend of thought – that is, liberalisation – among the masses, especially among the young people. Second, because this trend has found support from the sidelines. For example, there have been some comments from people in Hong Kong and Taiwan who are opposed to our Four Cardinal Principles and who think we should introduce the capitalist system lock, stock and barrel, as if that were the only genuine modernisation. What in fact is this liberalisation? It is an attempt to turn China's present policies in the direction of capitalism. The exponents of this trend are trying to lead us towards capitalism. That is why I have explained time and time again that our modernisation programme is a socialist one. *Our decision to apply the open policy and assimilate useful things from capitalist societies was made only to supplement the*

Modernisation of the PLA has included home-produced armoured personnel carriers and missile systems, like Hongjian 8 being launched from a Type 531 APC.

development of our socialist productive forces"
Emphasis added.

"We all remember that in 1980, after the defeat of the Gang of Four, the National People's Congress adopted a resolution to delete from the Constitution the provision concerning the right of citizens to "speak out freely, air their views fully, hold great debates and put up big-character posters". Why did we do this? Because there was an ideological trend of liberalisation. If that trend has been allowed to spread, it would have undermined our political stability and unity without which construction would be out of the question".

"It seems to me that the struggle against liberalisation will have to be carried on not only now but for the next 10 or 20 years. If we fail to

A firepower demonstration by NORINCO in 1988, with a main battle tank and Type 85 armoured personnel carrier with Type 82 multiple rocker launcher.

check this trend, it will merge with undesirable foreign things that will inevitably find their way into China because of our open policy and become a battering ram used against our modernisation programme. This is something we cannot afford to ignore. If you have read some of the comments that have been made by the people in Hong Kong and by bourgeois scholars in foreign countries, you will see that most of them insist that we should liberalise or say that there are no human rights in China. These commentators oppose the very things we believe in and hope that we will change. but we shall continue to raise problems and solve them in the light of the realities in China."

Remarks at the Sixth Plenary Session of the Party's Twelfth Central Committee 28 September 1986.

During the late 1930s and 1940s the Red Army had two enemies — the Guomindang and the Japanese. While participating in some military actions against both these opponents (and at times co-operating with the Guomindang against the Japanese) these military activities were not decisive in the conclusion of the war with Japan. The Red Army experienced a massive growth in numbers during the Second World War — from about forty thousand in 1937 to over one million in 1945. At the conclusion of the War it was much better prepared for its final conflict with the Guomindang, its resources having been boosted by captured stocks of Japanese military equipment. The Red Army had received some external aid, but its well-established policy of acquiring most of its equipment from its enemies remained. With the conclusion of the Second World War the Civil War resumed at great intensity, with the Communist forces now fielding large 'Field Armies'.

By 1948, communist propaganda, and the guerilla actions of the Red Army had weakened the Guomindang forces to such an extent that the Red Forces were able to regroup and go over to the offensive. Throughout the next year, the communists gained ground and equipment, through a series of successful attacks on Guomindang armies, until in April 1949, Chiang Kai-shek withdrew with his remaining forces to Taiwan.

The People's Republic of China was declared on 1 October 1949. The task of the PLA was now transformed from being a revolutionary army to a national force responsible for defence, internal security and reconstruction of a shattered economy. The army was used for a number of non-military tasks — to rebuild bridges, repair railways lines and ports and build roads. It was also required to consolidate Communist Party power throughout China.

The PLA's first military act after 1949 was to attempt to eliminate the last pocket of Guomindang resistance on Taiwan; this ended with the unsuccessful amphibious assaults on Quemoy and Matsu by units of the 3rd Field Army, which was repelled with significant losses to men and equipment.

The PLA gained control over Tibet in the summer of 1950, with very little active resistance encountered to the force of five divisions from 1st Field Army, and two divisions from 2nd Field Army which advanced into the country, forcing the Tibetan leader, the Dalai Lama, to accept Chinese rule.

Later that year, advancing United Nations forces in Korea, were judged a threat to mainland China. Chinese 'Volunteers' from the 38th, 39th, 40th, 42nd, 50th and 66th Field Armies (with three divisions in each army, each division with around ten thousand men) and later the 20th, 26th and 27th Field armies reinforced by divisions from the 30th Field army, crossed the borders with North Korea under the overall command of General (later Marshal) Peng Dehuai.

Chinese doctrine at this time, evolved during the civil war in China, called for infantry attacks at a place and time favourable to the nature of their light forces, avoiding contact until such a location could be found (an ambush, for example), and then attacking en-masse in an attempt to overwhelm the enemy. These tactics were initially used with great effectiveness against United Nations (principally United States) forces, driving them back down the Korean peninsular.

Chinese doctrine at this time also emphasised reliance on logistical support from the local population. In Korea this was lacking, and the armies were forced to rely on a small number of trucks and a vast number of coolies to maintain their lengthening supply lines. These were subject to aerial attack from United Nations aircraft, day and night, including carrier-borne aviation and long-range Super Fortress raids from Japan. Eventually the Chinese were forced to fight along a linear front against modern forces with superiority in fire power, communications, aerial support and logistics. The People's Liberation Army was deficient in all these areas, but its human wave

China has reached the nuclear and space age rather faster than many observers would have credited in the 1950s. These multi-stage missiles, seen in Tiananmen Square, are cited as being 'intercontinental'.

tactics were successful in its first three campaigns. There was enormous loss of life (casualty figures are still kept secret, but current Western estimates total about 450 thousand for the War) and by January-March 1951 during the fourth campaign Chinese forces were halted. PLA commanders realised that any possible success would depend upon a massive infusion of modern weapons and supplies, and training of their forces in their use. The Soviet Union supplied the PLA with artillery, radar-controlled anti-aircraft guns, aircraft, armour and logistical support.

By April 1953 the 'Chinese People's Volunteers' had undergone a significant transformation — they now were comprised of twenty-one corps, with corps artillery, nine artillery divisions, two armoured divisions and an air force of around 1800 aircraft. The Chinese Army had undergone an intense modernisation programme under the pressure of military conflict. This modernisation continued after the signing of the armistice which ended the Korean War, with Marshal Peng as Minister of National Defence and Vice Chairman of the National Defence Council.

Military co-operation with the Soviet Union increased under Marshal Peng, as he attempted to promote military professionalism, defence industrial production and modernisation of the PLA. He disagreed with Mao Zedong on the wisdom of Mao's Great Leap Forward — its 'backyard furnace' low-level industrialisation was damaging to the PLA's modernisation — and he was dismissed.

Mao preferred an army that was 'Red' —

Even though the PLA is some 2.3 million strong, the threat from force-multiplying chemical weapons is taken seriously. China has developed chemical weapons of its own and methods of protecting against them.

ideologically correct — rather than 'expert', that is to say professional and concerned more exclusively with military matters. This divergence in views on the correct strategy for the PLA continued to dog the army throughout the 1950s and 1960s, culminating in the misnamed Great Proletarian Cultural Revolution, a faction fight within the Party in which the PLA was finally forced to intervene to maintain stability.

The PLA's most recent drive for modernisation has been initiated by perceived potential threats from the soviet Union and Japan, and by the PLA's poor organisational and technological performance against Vietnam, and has been led by Deng Xiaoping, a former Chief of Staff of the PLA and a disgraced (and subsequently rehabilitated) victim of the Cultural Revolution. Under Deng Xiaoping the PLA has looked to the West (and with an eye on the Soviet Union) for military technology, equipment, training and information.

Chinese military production, previously organised for local consumption and ideological export from ministry — controlled plants and arsenals, has now been organised into commercially oriented state corporations; NORINCO (China North Industries Corporation) producing armoured fighting vehicles, ordnance, ammunition, and anti-tank missiles; CPMIEC (China Precision Machinery Import-Export Corporation), producing strategic and tactical missiles; CATIC (China Aviation Technology Import-Export Corporation) producing aircraft; CSSC (China State Ship Building Corporation), producing ships; CEIEC (China Electronic Import-Export Corporation), producing electronic equipment; CNEIC (China Nuclear Energy Industry Corporation), producing nuclear weapons, and the Great Wall Corporation. All of these corporations have responsibilities for local arms production for the PLA and arms export responsibilities where these are considered appropriate. China's urgent need for foreign exchange to finance its military modernisation programme has been responsible for a highly pragmatic policy on arms sales. Few clients are turned away.

China's modernisation programme has been characterised by an intense information gathering and analysis effort conducted by both military and civil organisations. The Academy of Military Sciences, for example, based on the North West outskirts of Beijing, has a large facility devoted entirely to the collection, translation and analysis of foreign military publications and data. The National Defence University, located nearby, also collects and analyses foreign military publications. These are only two of a number of military establishments seeking to expand China's technological resources. There are also a number of civil establishments, such as CDSTIC (The China Defence Science and Technology Information Centre) and the North Institute for Science and Technical Information (NISTI) which describes itself as follows:

"A comprehensive information research and documentation centre affiliated to the Ministry of Machine-Building and Electronics Industry of China."

It has more than 600 employees, of whom, approximately 70 per cent are scientific and technical personnel, including over 70 senior engineers and about 200 engineers. NISTI is engaged in information research, document service, technical consultation, editing and publishing books and periodicals, audio-visual service, and sponsoring exhibitions in aspects of science and technology, economy and market covering mechanics, optics, electronic, chemistry, material, manufacturing technology and defence industry and scientific research.

NISTI has stored up approximately one million copies of scientific and technical documents. It possesses advanced audio-video equipment, computerised laser typesetting system, colour printing equipment, document micrographics equipment and international on-line information retrieval terminals, and has fairly powerful information processing capability and modernised service means and methods."

Information collection centres throughout China undertake similar work to that of NISTI, subscribing to vast numbers of books, periodicals and specialist scientific and market studies, in a massive effort to help China leap-frog from a position of military and technical backwardness into the era of advanced technological warfare.

Three main phases of military development and modernisation can be identified in modern Chinese Communist history; the first involving the establishment and building of a communist armed force from scratch, with weapons and tactics being the product of improvisation; a second phase, in which Soviet equipment, organisation, doctrine and tactics were adopted, especially after the Korean War; and a third phase, beginning in the mid 1970s with the rehabilitation of hardline but modernist Deng Xiaoping. This phase has depended heavily on Western goodwill for its success, and China has been remarkably successful in persuading the West to sell it advanced weapons and technology and give it access to technical information. The massacre in Tiananmen Square has damaged this goodwill and trust, and shown that the PLA will hold itself back (or be held back) from its goal of modernisation and professionalism if it is used (or allows itself to be used) as an undisciplined, unprofessional force in domestic politics. The post-massacre efforts by the PLA to doctor history and deny that any such massacre occurred are not necessarily an indication of any remorse at the Army's actions but may be motivated by self-interest—the threat posed to modernisation by a boycott from the West. In the past the hardline policies of the Communist Party leadership and the PLA, as typified by the quoted remarks of Deng Xiaoping, have been an internal Chinese matter. Now, with dependence upon the West, such hard line policies are no longer acceptable.

Main Personalities

Since the disturbances in China began, there has been increasing interest in — and information on — those involved in both sides of the struggle. The list given here reflects those whose names have been mentioned in the media over the last few months and includes not only the leadership but also the dissidents and the protesters. It is, inevitably, a selective list and many of those who supported the pro-democracy movement and should have been mentioned have not been, simply because they did not receive the attention of the world's press.

A profile of the commanders of the seven military regions and a listing of PLA commanders are given in the following two sections.

Bian Hanwu
An unemployed worker who was sentenced to death in Shanghai on 15 June following a one-day trial. He is alleged to have "damaged transport facilities" on 6 June when a train was set on fire after it rammed demonstrators sitting on the tracks, killing six. Also sentenced to death at the same time were Xu Guoming and Yan Xuerong.

Chai Ling
Leader of the students at Tiananmen Square and a student at Beijing University. She made a tape recording of events in Tiananmen Square on the night of the massacre. Wife of Feng Congde. Now wanted by the Chinese authorities.

Chen Yun
One of the old time leadership and supporter of Premier Li Peng. Aged 84.

Chi Haotian
Chief of the General Staff and member of the Central Committee, who complained over the treatment of the PLA by civilians. He described this, before the problems in Tiananmen Square, as "an intolerable burden" and called for a concerted effort to remind China of the importance of the PLA. Reported on 1 June to be out of circulation because of his attitiude to martial law, he is now back on the political scene.

Chi Ling
Student leader and likely to be on the Chinese authorities wanted list of 21 dissidents.

Chou Liming
Vice-consul for culture in the Chinese consulate in San Francisco who requested political asylum on 10 June.

Deng Xiaoping

Senior Chinese leader. Born in 1904, Deng is from Guang'an county in the province of Sichuan in the south west of China. He studied in France and in the Soviet Union in 1926 and after 1927 held successively the posts of army political commissar, director of the political department of an army group and deputy director of the General Political Department. Deng took part in the Long March and was political commissar of the 129th Division of the Eighth Route Army after 1937, political commissar of the Second Field Army during the Chinese Revolutionary War (War of Liberation) 1946-49, and political commissar of the Southwest China Military Area after 1949. He was vice-chairman of the Military Commission of the CPC (Communist Party of China) Central Committee and Chief of the General Staff of the PLA in 1975. He became chairman of the Military Commission of the CPC Central Committee in June 1981 and chairman of the Central Military Commission in June 1983. In April 1976 he was denounced as 'an unrepentant capitalist roadster' and removed from office, although this fall from grace did not last.

General Hong Zuezhi (second from left) and General Liu Huaqing (third from right) at a visit to the Satellite Launching Centre. General Hong is director of the logistics department which controls the weapon arsenals; General Liu is a member of the Central Military Commission.

Deng Yingchao
Widow of former premier Chou En-Lai and one of the old time leadership. Supporter of Premier Li Peng.

Ding Guangen
Alternate member of the Politburo.

Fang Lizhi
Dissident astrophysicist who took refuge in the US Embassy with his family because of the fear of reprisals by the Chinese authorities. The authorities later closed the borders, saying "Fang Lizhi and Li Shuxian together engaged in counter-revolutionary propaganda and instigation. They are guilty and they escaped from justice. All points of exit from China should be on their guard for them." At one time vice president of the University of Science and Technology in the central Chinese city of Hefei, Fang has been a promoter of greater democracy in China for some time. However, after the fall from power of Hu Yaobang in January 1987, Fang was expelled from the party and transferred to work as a professor in the Beijing Observatory.

Feng Congde
Husband of Chai Ling, who led the students at Tiananmen Square. Now wanted by the Chinese authorities.

Gua Haifeng
Student leader and secretary of the independent students' group. Arrested by the Chinese authorities on 10 June.

Hong Xuezhi
General Hong is a member of the Military Commission and director of the logistics department which controls the weapon arsenals. As such, he probably has some control over China's nuclear weapons. He was born in 1913 in Jinzhai county, Anhui province and joined the communist party in 1929 at the age of only 16.

Hu Qili

Moderate member of the Politburo who has not been seen in recent weeks. Likely to be dismissed along with Zhao Ziyang.

Hu Yaobang
Former member of the Politburo and deposed Communist Party leader whose death on 15 April was one of the catalysts for the present unrest.

Jia Zhijie
Governor of the province of Lanzhou, who threatened to kill anyone who interfered with the infrastructure of the province.

Jiang Zhemin
Party secretary for Shanghai and a member of the Politburo. Generally disliked by the ordinary citizens of Shanghai.

Li Dan
The announcer at Radio Beijing who made a radio announcement early on 4 June saying thousands had been killed in Tiananmen Square. He was arrested immediately after the broadcast.

Li Desheng
Former commander of the Shenyang military region and now influential among the leadership.

Li Lu
Student leader at Peking University, and now probably on the Chinese authorities wanted list.

Li Peng

Prime minister of China and adopted son of Deng Yingohao, widow of Zhou Enlai. His father, Li Shuoxun, was executed by the Kuomintang in 1931 when Li Peng was three. Li's mother, Zhao Juntao, was one of the first members of the Communist Party. Her sister was a friend of Zhou Enlai; at one stage Zhou even cared for Li Peng.

Li Ruihuan
Member of the Politburo.

Li Shuxian
Wife of Fang Lizhi, who took refuge with him in the US Embassy. Assistant professor at Beijing University.

Li Tieying
Member of the Politburo.

Li Xiannian

Former president. One of the old time leadership and supporter of Premier Li Peng. Aged 80.

Li Ximing
Member of the Politburo.

Liu Gang
Said to have assisted the students in Tiananmen Square from behind the scenes. Now wanted by the Chinese authorities.

Ma Qiuyun
Chinese diplomat based in Tokyo who asked for political asylum.

Ma Shaofang
One of 21 people wanted by the Chinese authorities who gave himself up on 16 June.

Nie Rongzhen
Marshal Nie, born 1899, is vice-chairman of the Communist Party's Military Commission and is said to be influential with the leadership. From Pingjin county, Sichuan province, Nie has held a wide variety of positions in the PLA and is vice-chairman of the Central Military Commission. He is alos the honarary chairman of the China Inventors' Association and Honorary Chairman of the National Committee on Ageing.

Ning Honshan
Second secretary in the educational section of the Chinese Embassy in London who asked for political asylum on 11 June.

Peng Zhen
One of the old time leadership and supporter of Premier Li Peng. Aged 87.

No longer united. From left to right are Zhao Ziyang, President Yang Shangkun and Premier Li Peng. Even in this picture, taken on 4 April 1989, Zhao seems to be set apart from the main leadership.

Qiao Shi

One of the five members of the standing committee of the Politburo and tipped to be the new leader of the party following the removal of Zhao Ziyang. Qiao is the party's top internal security officer, as head of the Leading Group for Political and Legal Affairs. Born in the Shejiang province near Shanghai, Qiao is also secretary of the Political and Legal Commission, and head of the Central Foreign Affairs Group. He is understood to have been involved in China's intelligence services, possibly as head. His son is studying at Cambridge; his son's wife works for the BBC Chinese programme. As at 17 June he was being tipped as a close ally of premier Li Peng. Aged 65.

Qin Jiwei

Minister of Defence and Politburo member who may have been removed from power for failing to support martial law but now seems to be back at his desk. Minister of National Defence for the Navy. Aged 74.

Rui Xingwen

Member of the Secretariat.

Song Ping

Member of the Politburo.

Tian Jiyun

Once known as a supporter of the discredited Zhao Ziyang, Tian (a member of the politburo) was seen on television in the second week of June praising the military crackdown and visiting wounded soldiers.

Wan Li

Chairman of the standing committee of the National People's Congress and Politburo member. At one time regarded as a moderate, Wan was seen on television on 9 June with Deng Xiaoping and Li Peng praising the conduct of the troops in Tiananmen Square. Aged 73.

Wang Dan

One of several leading student activists whose whereabouts is now unknown, although there are unconfirmed reports that Wang was shot and bayoneted to death by soldiers in Tiananmen Square on 4 June. According to the *Sunday Times* of 11 June, just before troops advanced, he made an impassioned pleas to fellow students to withdraw, arguing that the best way to serve democracy in China was by surviving rather than dying a martyr. Wang was a student at Beijing University. Later reports indicate that Wang was among a group of 21 activists who had been put on the 'wanted' list by the Chinese authorities. The photograph above shows him (right) talking on 2 May with a government spokesman, Li Zhotian

Wang Weilin

The 19 year old student who was seen on television stopping a column of tanks simply by standing in front of them. Wang, the son of a Beijing factory worker, is now believed to have been executed.

Wang Zhen

Vice-premier since 1975 and one of the old time leadership, Wang was deputy chief of the general staff in 1955 and hence has close links with some of China's senior generals. Supporter of Premier Li Peng. The only one among the present leadership who was not purged during the Cultural Revolution he is a strong believer in the old revolutionary values, having joined the party in May 1927. He was born in Hunan province, near the home town of Mao Zedong. The photograph shows him in 1985 at the groundbreaking ceremony for Beijing's first golf course, built with Japanese help.

Wen Jiabao

Alternate member of the Secretariat, the party General Office. Ally of Zhao Ziyang and therefore at risk of being purged by the hardliners.

Wu Xueqian
Vice-premier and member of the Politburo who is believed to be out of favour. A former foreign minister, Wu was absent from a party and military gathering held on 9 June. Aged 67.

Wuer Kaixi
One of 21 students wanted for questioning by the Chinese authorities, his picture was shown extensively on television in China in the second week of June, apparently in an attempt to encourage people to turn him over to the authorities. Wuer, 21, took part in a televised debate — in his pyjamas — with Premier Li Peng in the early stages of the hunger strike in Tiananmen Square. A member of the Ulghur moslem minority, Wuer distinguished himself as a highly competent orator at Tiananmen Square.

Xiao Ke
General Xiao, formerly of the General Staff, is rumoured to be one of the 'power brokers' who could remove Deng Xiaoping from power.

Xiong Wei
One of the 21 student leaders wanted by the Chinese authorities. Arrested on 14 June while on a train, having been betrayed by his mother. A law student at Beijing University.

Xu Guoming
Shanghai brewery employee who was sentenced to death in Shanghai on 15 June following a one-day trial. He is alleged to have "damaged transport facilities" on 6 June when a train was set on fire after it rammed demonstrators sitting on the tracks, killing six. Also sentenced to death at the same

The names and fate of many pro-democracy demonstrators will never be known, the only record of their efforts being photographs like this.

time were Bian Hanwu and Yan Xuerong.

Xu Xiangqian

Marshal Xu, born 1901, is a former defence minister and is rumoured to be one of the 'power brokers' who could remove Deng Xiaoping from power. A native of Wutai county, Shanxi province, Xu entered the Huangpu Military Academy in 1924 and became commander of the Fourth Front Army of the Red Army in November 1931. He later took part in the Long March. Has held the position of vice-chairman of the Central Military Commission.

Yan Mingfu

Member of the Secretariat.

Yan Yuerong

A worker at a Shanghai radio factory who was sentenced to death in Shanghai on 15 June following a one-day trial. He is alleged to have "damaged transport facilities" on 6 June when a train was set on fire after it rammed demonstrators sitting on the tracks, killing six. Also sentenced to death at the same time were Bian Hanwu and Xu Guoming.

Yang Baibing

General Yang is the younger brother of Yang Shangkun and is head of the political department of the PLA. Yang was promoted ahead of several senior generals to this position. His son, General Yang Jianhua, commands the 27th Group Army.

Yang Dezhi

General Yang, once Chief of Staff, is rumoured to be one of the 'power brokers' who could remove Deng Xiaoping from power. Born in 1910 in Zhuzhou city, Hunan province, Yang has held a number of appointments in the army. These include chief of staff of the Chinese People's Volunteers in Korea in 1951 and commander of first the Wuhan and then the Kunming military regions in the 1970s. He has been deputy secretary general of the Central Military Commission since 1983.

Yang Jianhua

Commander of the 27th Field Army, son of General Yang Baibing and nephew of General Yang Shungkun.

Yang Rudai

Moderate member of the Politburo and party leader of the Sichuan province; associate of Zhao Ziyang who is likely to be dismissed because of this connection.

Yang Shangkun

President of China since 1988 and Politburo member who is said to have the loyalty of troops of the 27th Army which he once commanded. Likely to become the Vice Chairman of the Military Affairs Commission. Aged 82, Yang is a veteran of the Long March who has held a wide variety of military posts. He joined the communist party in 1926, at the age of 19, becoming director of the propaganda department in Jiangsu province in 1931.

Yang Tao

One of the 21 student leaders wanted by the Chinese authorities. Arrested on 17 June, Yang, 19, was a history student at Beijing University.

Yao Yilin

Senior vice president and member of the Standing Committee of the Politburo who has said that he would not be concerned if the Western industrial nations decided not to invest in China. As at 17 June he was being cited as a close ally of Premier Li Peng, along with Qiao Shi.

Yao Yongzhan

Hong Kong student whose arrest at Shanghai airport on 11 June as he was trying to leave has led to added diplomatic friction between the UK and China. David Gilmore, a spokesman for the British Foreign Office said that "any maltreatment by the Chinese authorities of the Hong Kong Chinese would have the most damaging impact on confidence in Hong Kong". Yao is accused of being a leader of the Autonomous Union of Shanghai Universities and Colleges, which the Chinese authorities want disbanded.

Yuan Mu

State Council's spokesman who has stated that "troops did not kill a single student or individual". He has also said that foreign countries should not take a short term view of events and that China would not be influenced by condemnation from abroad.

Zhang Aiping

General Zhang was born in 1908 in Daxian county, Sichuan county. A former minister of defence, Zhang was one of the seven senior officers who wrote to the People's Daily in May saying that the army belonged to the people and must never be used against the people. Like many others of the senior Chinese leaders, Zhang is a veteran of the Long March.

Zhang Limin

Member of the Chinese consulate in San Francisco who requested political asylum on 10 June.

Zhang Lin

A 1988 graduate of Qinqhua University who was arrested on 14 June, supposedly for having had contacts with dissident astrophysicist Fang Lizhi. After leaving university, Zhang reportedly returned to his home town of Benbu in Anhui province to set up an educational program for students and workers. In an interview two months ago, Zhang is said to have complained that he was unable to see Fang and was only able to see his wife, Li Shuxian.

Zhao Ziyang

Disgraced member of the Politburo Standing Committee who was stripped of power in May and has not been seen since 19 May. Vice chairman to Deng Xiaoping on the all-important Military Commission which cut the PLA. Internal party documents circulating among senior officials in the second week of June criticise Zhao but do not accuses him of being a revolutionary. According to The New York Times, there are three specific criticisms being levelled against him: that he helped organise the student mourning for the former leader, Hu Yaobang, whose death on 15 April started the movement; that his words and actions encouraged the student movement; that he violated party discipline, by saying things that he should not have done. Zhao, at the age of 69, is a relative youngster.

Zheng Tuobin

Minister of Foreign Economic Relations and Trade who said on 15 June that China would "make necessary struggles if foreign partners use the crackdown on riots as an excuse to cancel, suspend or postpone their obligations."

Zhou Fengsuo

One of 21 student leaders whose pictures were broadcast on Chinese television as being wanted by the Chinese authorities. Arrested the day after the broadcast, Zhou was said to have been turned in by his sister and brother-in-law in the city of Xian, 750 km south west of Beijing. Before the unrest, Zhou was studying Physics at Qinqhua University in Beijing.

Zhu Rong Ji

Mayor of Shanghai whose skilled manoeuvring helped to contain unrest in the city.

Regional Commanders

One of the first steps in the streamlining and modernisation of the PLA was to cut the number of Military Regions from eleven to seven. This, in the words of a sophisticated Commander, "got rid of four 'mini-Pentagons'". With notable exceptions the Commanders today are young by Chinese standards, that is, in their mid to late fifties. Since ranks were restored they are all Lieutenant Generals and, with one exception, all members of the Central Committee of the Communist Party. They have all given public support to President Yang Shangkun in his implementation of Martial Law and all are known to be supporters of Deng Xiaoping. Currently there is no news on who is likely to replace Chi Haotian, who has been Chief of the General Staff since November 1987 but is now in disgrace with Zhao Ziyang.

Lt Gen Li Jiulong who commands the Jinan Military Region has been in military service for over 40 years. He joined the Army during the war against Japan and later fought in the Liberation War in the Tianjin area. He took part in the Korean War as well as the brief border war with India in 1962. He appears to have "kept his head down and his mouth shut" during the Cultural Revolution and became a deputy Divisional Commander in Chengdu. Li was one of the senior Commanders in the Sino-Vietnamese War of 1979. He is well known for his contributions to the *Liberation Army Daily* and as a lecturer on military history and strategy.

Lt Gen Zhou Yibing was named Commander of the Beijing Military Region in April 1988 when he replaced Qin Jiwei who became Defence Minister. Little or nothing is known about his youth except that Zhou like many senior cadres (officers) have followed the Maoist line of painstakingly keeping their names out of the press. He is 58 and was first noted as an efficient Chief of Staff to a Maoist Field Army in the Beijing Military Region in April, 1964. Zhou survived the Cultural Revolution without trouble and became a PLA deputy to the 6th National People's Congress in 1983. At the time he was attending a senior Military Academy in Beijing. Around January 1987 Zhou was appointed Deputy Commander to the Beijing Military Region.

Lt Gen Zhang Wannian was appointed as Military

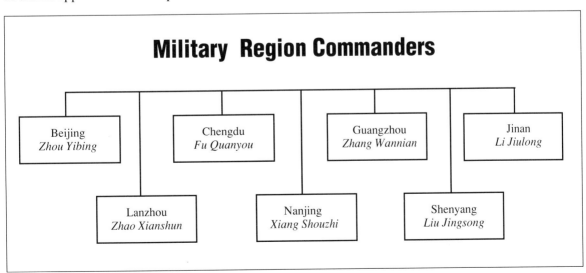

Military Region Commanders

Beijing *Zhou Yibing*	Chengdu *Fu Quanyou*	Guangzhou *Zhang Wannian*	Jinan *Li Jiulong*
	Lanzhou *Zhao Xianshun*	Nanjing *Xiang Shouzhi*	Shenyang *Liu Jingsong*

Commander of the important Guangzhou Military Region shortly after the 13th Party Congress in 1987. Earlier he had served as a Deputy Commander in the Wuhan Military Region. Little is known about Zhang except that he is beloved by the troops and close to Deng Xiaoping.

General Xiang Shouzhi is 72 and has been in command of the Nanjing Military Region since 1987. Xiang joined the Chinese Workers' and Peasants Red Army in 1934 and became a deputy platoon leader before taking part in the Long March of 1935. Later he served in the war against Japan and commanded a company in the famous 129 Division of the famous 8th Route Army. During the War of Liberation he served with Qin Jiwei who is still Defence Minister and after it became Chief of Staff in one of the Maoist Field Armies. It is not known what happened to him during the Cultural Revolution but he emerged afterwards as a senior cadre in the 2nd Artillery which later assumed responsibility for nuclear weapons. He is one of Deng Xiaoping's favourite 'cronies' and has the reputation for being an efficient Commander.

Lt Gen Fu Quanyou is Commander of the Chengdu Military Region and at 59 has earned himself a name as a 'scholarly general' after writing articles in the Military Science Journal on how to organise frontal attacks. He has since written for the Liberation Army Daily on troops management and "the basic spirit of Army building in the new period" of modernisation. He apparently owes his present prominence to his war record on the Yunnan front in 1984/5 but little or nothing has been disclosed about his personal exploits.

Lt Gen Liu Jingsong, who Commands the vital Shenyang Military Region in the extreme north east gained his war experience in "helping Vietnam to fight against the United States in the sixties." Unlike other commanders it is known that he was one of seven children and that his 73 year old father – a peasant – is still alive. But the details of his family life end there. However, Liu became "an outstanding student" at the infantry school and since that time has specialised in commanding mechanised units beginning as a platoon commander. He is also a good administrator and "can fire artillery as well as drive a car." His region still contains the most important industrial plant in China as well as the largest oil field.

Lt Gen Zhao Xianshun who commands the Lanzhou Military Region is known to have served in the Shenyang Military Region from 1976 to 1984. But little else is known of this general before he assumed his present Command.

At some point Military Commanders must give in to the fact that their troops, as well as foreigners, would like to know something about their backgrounds. But, currently, neither Military Attachés in Beijing nor the troops themselves have any interesting details about their lives.

PLA Commanders

PEOPLE'S LIBERATION ARMY LEADERSHIP

General Logistics Department of the People's Liberation Army

Director	Zhao Nanqi
Deputy Directors	Liu Mingpu
	Wen Yuanchun
	Zhang Bin
	Zong Shunliu
Political Commissar	Liu Anyuan
Chief of Staff	Zong Shunliu
Deputy Chiefs of Staff	Liu Lumin
	Wen Guangchun

Armaments Department

Director	Liu Liankun

Foreign Affairs Department

Director	Zhang Shiyan

General Political Department of the People's Liberation Army

Director	Yang Baibing
Deputy Directors	Guo Linxiang
	Zhou Keyu
	Zhou Wenyuan
	Zhu Yunqian

General Staff Department of the People's Liberation Army

Chief of Staff	Chi Haotian
Assistant to the Chief of Staff	Liu Kai
Deputy Chiefs of Staff	Han Huaizhi
	He Qizong
	Xu Huizi
	Xu Xin

Admiral Ma Xinchun, left, commander of China's North Sea Fleet picture in 1986 on the visit of three vessels of the US Pacific Fleet to Qingdao Naval Base.

Foreign Affairs Bureau
Director   Song Wenzhong
Deputy Directors   Fu Jiaping
                                                  Yu Jianzhong

Armaments Department
Director   He Pengfei

National Defence Science, Technology and Industry Commission

(Created from merger of National Defence Industry Office, National Defence Science and Technology Commission, and Office of the Science, Technology and Armament Commission of the Military Commission, August 1982; subordinate to the State Council and both the State and Party Military Commissions)

Chairman   Ding Henggao
                                                  Shen Rongjun
                                                  Xie Guang
                                                  Wu Shaozu
Political Commissar

Foreign Affairs Bureau
Director   Li Xiaolin
Deputy Director   Cheng Lusheng
United States Division Director   Zhang Wenxiao

PEOPLE'S LIBERATION ARMY SERVICE ARMS

Air Force

Commander	Wang Hai
Deputy Commanders	Li Yongtai
	Lin Hu
	Yu Zhenwu
Political Commissar	Zhu Guang
Deputy Political Commissar	Gao Xingmin
Chief of Staff	Yu Zemin
Deputy Chiefs of Staff	Chen Huiting
	Xin Dianfeng

Navy

Commander	Zhang Lianzhong
Deputy Commanders	Li Jing
	Zhang Xusan
Political Commissar	Li Yaowen
Deputy Political Commissar	Wei Jinshan
Chief of Staff	Zhang Xusan
Deputy Chief of Staff	Wang Zuyao

Second Artillery Corps

(Also known as Chinese Strategic Rocket Force)

Commander	Li Xuge
Deputy Commanders	Li Maozhi
	Yang Guoliang
	Yang Huan
Political Commissar	Liu Lifeng
Deputy Political Commissar	Yin Fatang

Organisational Chart of the Air Force

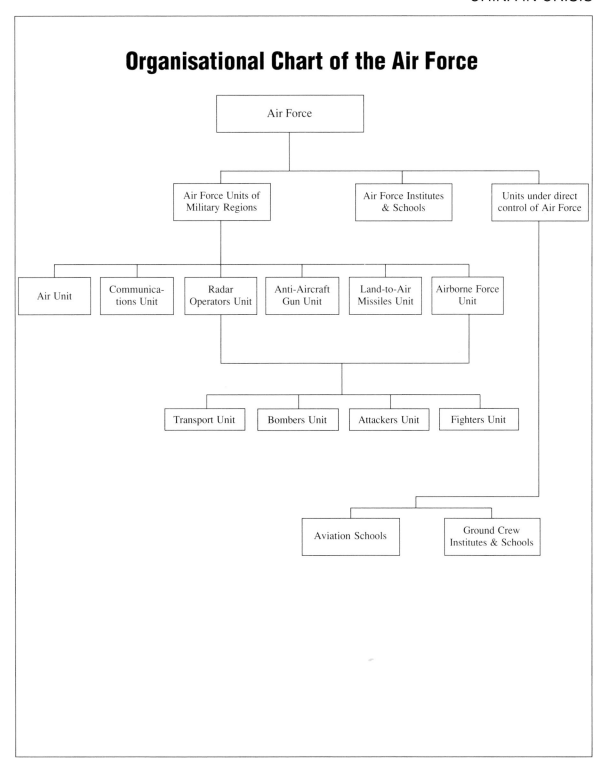

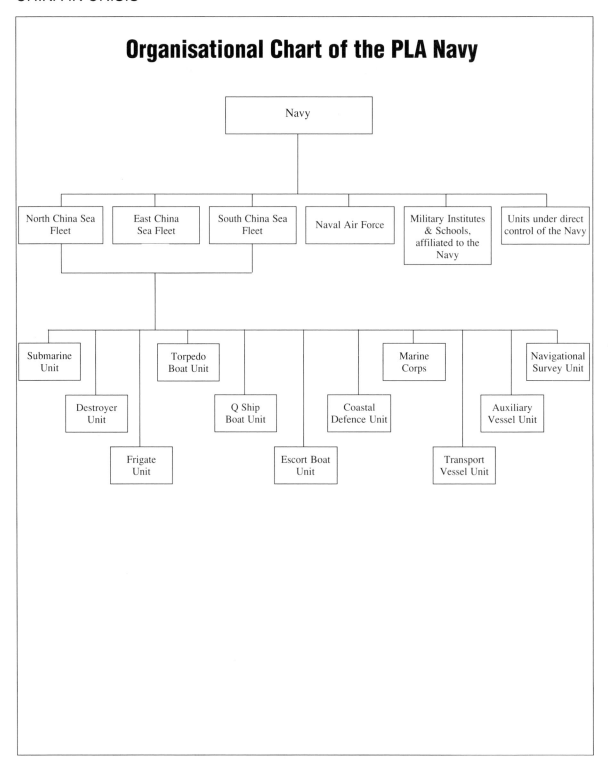

Organisational Chart of the PLA Navy

Navy

- North China Sea Fleet
- East China Sea Fleet
- South China Sea Fleet
- Naval Air Force
- Military Institutes & Schools, affiliated to the Navy
- Units under direct control of the Navy

- Submarine Unit
- Destroyer Unit
- Frigate Unit
- Torpedo Boat Unit
- Q Ship Boat Unit
- Escort Boat Unit
- Coastal Defence Unit
- Transport Vessel Unit
- Marine Corps
- Auxiliary Vessel Unit
- Navigational Survey Unit

Organisational Chart of the
Chinese People's Liberation Army

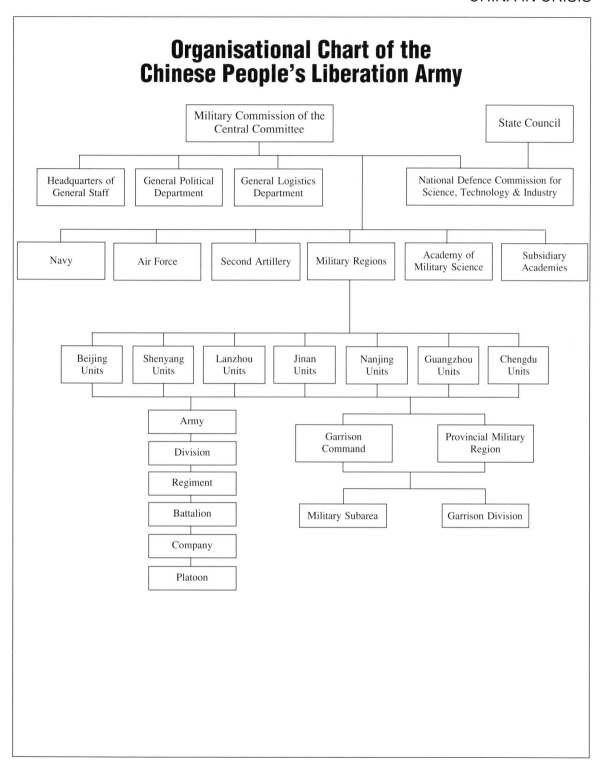

MILITARY REGIONS

Beijing Military Region
(Includes Hebei, Nei Monggol and Shanxi Military Districts)

Beijing Regional Headquarters
Commander	Zhou Yibing
Deputy Commanders	Li Laizhu
	Liu Yudi
	Pan Yan
	Yan Tongmao
	Zhou Yiyong
Political Commissar	Liu Zhenhua

Hebei Military District
Commander	Dong Xuelin
First Political Commissar	Xing Chongzhi
Political Commissar	Zhang Chao

Nei Monggol Military District
Commander	Cai Ying
Deputy Commander	Fang Chenghai
Political Commissar	Liu Yiyuan
Shanxi Military District	
Commander	Yu Hongli
Deputy Commander	Dong Yunhai
First Political Commissar	Li Ligong
Political Commissar	Luo Jinghui

Beijing Garrison
Commander	Yan Tongmao
Deputy Commanders	He Shangchun
	Wei Yingji
First Political Commissar	Li Ximing
Political Commissar	Li Jinmin

Tianjin Garrison
Commander	Zheng Guozhong
Deputy Commander	He Yanran
First Political Commissar	Li Ruihuan
Political Commissar	Lan Baojing

BEIJING MILITARY REGION

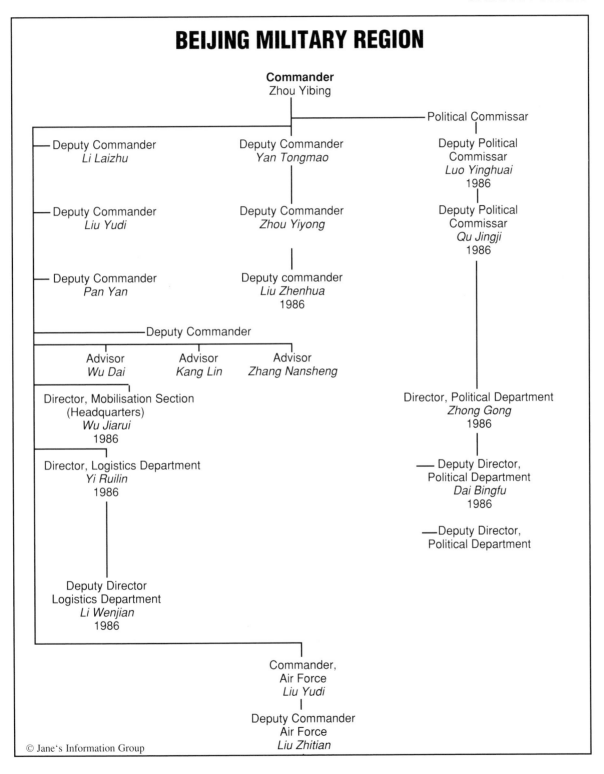

Commander
Zhou Yibing

Political Commissar

Deputy Commander
Li Laizhu

Deputy Commander
Yan Tongmao

Deputy Political
Commissar
Luo Yinghuai
1986

Deputy Commander
Liu Yudi

Deputy Commander
Zhou Yiyong

Deputy Political
Commissar
Qu Jingji
1986

Deputy Commander
Pan Yan

Deputy commander
Liu Zhenhua
1986

Deputy Commander

Advisor
Wu Dai

Advisor
Kang Lin

Advisor
Zhang Nansheng

Director, Mobilisation Section
(Headquarters)
Wu Jiarui
1986

Director, Political Department
Zhong Gong
1986

Director, Logistics Department
Yi Ruilin
1986

Deputy Director,
Political Department
Dai Bingfu
1986

Deputy Director,
Political Department

Deputy Director
Logistics Department
Li Wenjian
1986

Commander,
Air Force
Liu Yudi

Deputy Commander
Air Force
Liu Zhitian

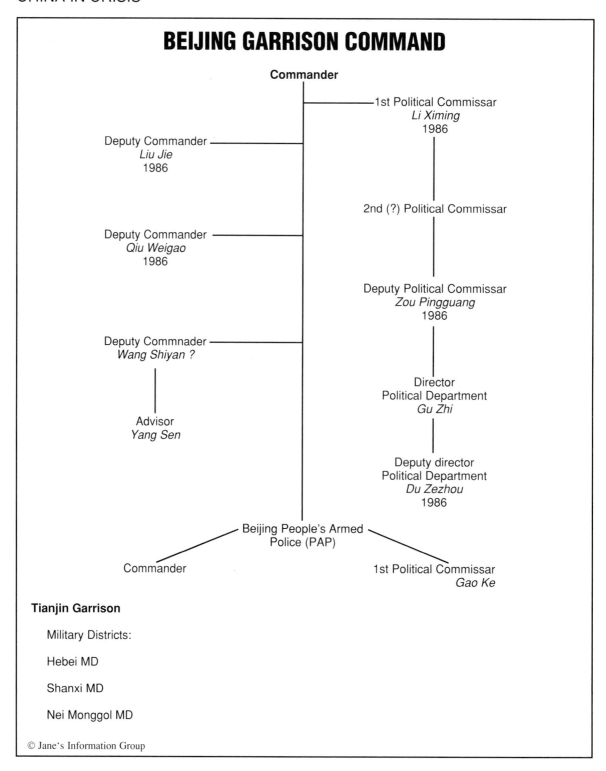

BEIJING GARRISON COMMAND

Commander

1st Political Commissar
Li Ximing
1986

Deputy Commander
Liu Jie
1986

2nd (?) Political Commissar

Deputy Commander
Qiu Weigao
1986

Deputy Political Commissar
Zou Pingguang
1986

Deputy Commnader
Wang Shiyan ?

Director
Political Department
Gu Zhi

Advisor
Yang Sen

Deputy director
Political Department
Du Zezhou
1986

Beijing People's Armed
Police (PAP)

Commander

1st Political Commissar
Gao Ke

Tianjin Garrison

Military Districts:

Hebei MD

Shanxi MD

Nei Monggol MD

© Jane's Information Group

Chengdu Military Region
(Includes Guizhou, Sichuan, Xizang and Yunnan Military Districts)

Chengdu Regional Headquarters
Commander	Fu Quanyou
Deputy Commanders	Hou Shujun
	Liao Xilong
	Ma Bingchen
	Zhang Taiheng
Political Commissar	Wan Haifeng

Guizhou Military District
Commander	Jiao Bin
First Political Commissar	Hu Jintao
Political Commissar	Kang Huzhen
Sichuan Military District	
Commander	Zhang Changshun
Deputy Commanders	Cong Chengde
	Ding Zhaoqian
First Political Commissar	Yang Rudai
Political Commissar	Gao Shuchun

Xizang Military District
Commander	Jiang Hongquan
Deputy Commanders	Gao Changjin
	Liu Yongkang
	Zhang Fengjiao
First Political Commissar	Wu Jinghua
Political Commissar	Zhang Shaosong

Yunnan Military District
Commander	Wang Zuxun
Deputy Commanders	Sun Peiting
	Zhao Yongmao
First Political Commissar	Pu Chaozhu
Political Commissar	Zhao Kun

Guangzhou Military Region
(Includes Guangdong, Guangxi, Hainan, Hubei and Hunan Military Districts)

Guangzhou Regional Headquarters
Commander   Zhang Wannian
Deputy Commanders   Liu Cunzhi
  Liu Hejiao
Political Commissar   Zhang Zhongxian

Guangdong Military District
Commander   Zhang Juhui
Deputy Commander   Wen Guoqing
First Political Commissar   Lin Ruo
Political Commissar   Xiu Xianghui

Guangxi Military District
Commander   Li Xinliang
Deputy Commanders   Li Licheng
  Zhao Yunling
First Political Commissar   Chen Huiguang
Political Commissar   Xiao Xuchu

Hainan Military District
Commander   Pang Weiqiang
Deputy Commander   Lai Ziying
Political Commissar   Liu Guinan

Hubei Military District
Commander   Wang Shen
Deputy Commander   Chen Zuocai
First Political Commissar   Guan Guangfu
Political Commissar   Zhang Xueqi

Hunan Military District
Commander   Jiang Jinliu
Deputy Commander   Xiao Qiuru
Political Commissar   Gu Shanqing

Jinan Military Region
(Includes Henan and Shandong Military Districts)

Jinan Regional Headquarters
Commander   Li Jiulong
Deputy Commanders   Gu Hui
  Lin Jigui

	Ma Weizhi
	Ma Xinchun
	Zhang Zhijian
Political Commissar	Song Quingwei

Henan Military District
Commander	Zhan Jingwu
First Political Commissar	Yang Xizong
Political Commissars	Dong Guoqing
	He Jinqu

Shandong Military District
Commander	Liu Yude
Deputy Commanders	Yan Zhuo
	Zheng Guangchen
First Political Commissar	Liang Buting

Lanzhou Military Region
(Includes Gansu, Ningxia, Qinghai, Shaanxi and Xinjiang Military Districts)

Lanzhou Regional Headquarters
Commander	Zhao Xianshun
Deputy Commander	Dong Zhanlin
Political Commissar	Li Xuanhua

Gansu Military District
Commander	Zhou Yucchi
Deputy Commander	He Zhiyang
First Political Commissar	Li Ziqi
Political Commissar	Wen Jinyi

Ningxia Military District
Commander	Liu Xueji
Political Commissar	Wang Huanmin

Qinghai Military District
Commander	Qui Shuxian
Deputy Commander	Jie Zhanbin
First Political Commissar	Yin Kesheng
Political Commissar	Lu Baoyin

Shaanxi Military District

Commander	Wang Xibin
Deptuy Commander	Wang Zhicheng
Political Commissars	Kong Shaowen
	Zhao Huanzhi

Xinjiang Military District

Commander	Gao Huanchang
Deputy Commanders	Li Zhenzhong
	Wang Ke
	Zhang Defu
First Political Commissar	Song Hanliang
Political Commissars	Tan Shanhe
	Tang Guangcai

Nanjing Military Region

(Includes Anhui, Fujian, Jiangsu, Jiangxi and Zhejiang Military Districts)

Nanjing Regional Headquarters

Commander	Xiang Shouzhi
Deputy Commanders	Guo Tao
	Nie Kuiju
	Wang Chengbin
Political Commissar	Fu Kuiqing

Anhui Military District

Commander	Li Yuanxi
Deputy Commanders	Guo Shengkun
	Zhang Jinbao
	Zhong Tingpeng
Political Commissar	Zhang Linyuan

Fujian Military District

Commander	Zhang Zongde
Deputy Commanders	Chen Shuqing
	Shi Rongji
First Political Commissar	Chen Guangyi
Political Commissar	Cong Lizhi

Jiangsu Military District

Commander   Zhen Shen
Deputy Commanders   Chen Yuexing
     Wang Tailan
First Political Commissar   Han Peixin
Political Commissars   Ye Guozheng
     Yue Dewang

Jiangxi Military District

Commander   Wang Baotian
Deputy Commanders   Shen Shanwen
     Shen Wenqiang
Political Commissar   Wang Guande

Zhejiang Military District

Commander   Li Qing
Deputy Commanders   Wang Wenhui
     Yan Baofu
     Yang Shijie
First Political Commissar   Wang Fang
Political Commissar   Liu Xinzeng

Shanghai Garrison

Commander   Ba Zhongtan
Deputy Commander   Ren Yonggui
Political Commissars   Ping Changxi
     Yang Zhifan

Shenyang Military Region

(Includes Heilongjiang, Jilin and Liaoning Military Districts)

Shenyang Regional Headquarters

Commander   Liu Jingsong
Deputy Commanders   Shi Baoyuan
     Zhu Dunfa
Political Commissar   Song Keda

Heilongjiang Military District

Commander   Shao Zhao
Deputy Commander   Yu Dianchen
First Political Commissar   Sun Weiben
Political Commissar   Ma Chunwa

PRC Military Organisation 1988

```
                        ┌──────────────────┐
                        │     DEFENCE      │
                        │     MINISTRY     │
                        ├──────────────────┤
                        │  PLA Chief of    │
                        │  General Staff   │
                        └──────────────────┘
```

DEFENCE MINISTRY — PLA Chief of General Staff

ARMY HQ
- FORCES: Infantry, Armor, Artillery, Mountain Operations
- CORPS: Aviation, Signal Engineer, Anti-Chemical Warfare
- SPECIAL UNITS: Electronic Counter-Measures, Meteorlogical

NAVY HQ
- FLEETS: North, East, South
- FORCES: Aviation, Coastal Defence
- CORPS: Marine

AIRFORCE HQ
- SPECIAL UNITS: Anti-Aircraft Missile & Artillery, Paratroops, Radar & Electronic Counter-Measure

STRATEGIC NUCLEAR COMMAND
- FORCES: Submarine
- CORPS: Strategic Rocket
- SPECIAL UNITS: Aviation

Order of Battle

During June 1989, more information than previously known has become available on the order of battle of the PLA Army. Press reports initially mis-identified several units and their military region subordination. The following information is the best available and represents a significant step forward in Western understanding of the PLA command structure.

The basic hierarchy begins with the seven military regions which are sub-divided again into 29 military districts on a provincial basis. In addition there are three Garrison Commands, one each in Beijing, Shanghai and an unidentified location. A single independent military district exists surrounding Beijing.

Although many units cannot be identified, it is understood that there are 80 Infantry Divisions (some are classified as Mechanised Divisions), 10 Armoured (Tank) Divisions and about six Artillery Divisions. There are 50 independent engineer regiments and some independent artillery regiments, many specialising in anti-aircraft artillery.

Following the 1988 re-organisation, the former Field Armies were redefined as Group Armies with integral artillery, engineer, air and other support. A Group Army is equivalent to a NATO Corps and represents a nominal strength of between 50 000 and 56 000 troops.

Group Army Locations

Group Army	Military Districts	Military Region
1	Nanjing	Nanjing
12	Nanjing	Nanjing
14	Sichuan	Chengdu
15	Wuhan	Guangzhou
16	Shenyang	Shenyang
21	Lanzhou	
24	Nei Monggol	Beijing
27	Shijiazhuang	Beijing
28	Hebei(?)	Beijing(?)
38	Beijing	Beijing
39	Shenyang	Shenyang
40	Shenyang	Shenyang
54	?	Jinan
63	?	?
64	-	Shenyang
65	-	Beijing
66	-	Beijing
67	?	?

Independent Divisions

1 Tank	Hebei (Tianjin)	Beijing
6 Tank	Beijin	Beijing
15 Airborne	Wuhan	Guangzhou

Notes: 16th Group Army is said to be of uncertain loyalty; 24th Group Army is headquartered at Chengde in Nei Monggol (Inner Mongolia); 27th Group Army has been moved from Hebei to Beijing to support the Garrison Command; 28th Group Army is said to be of uncertain loyalty; 38th Group Army comprises 112th Infantry Division (Xinching), 113th Mechanised Division (Boaching) and 114th Infantry Division (Ding Xian/Hebei); 40th Group Army is said to be of uncertain loyalty; 63rd Group Army is said to be of uncertain loyalty; 66th Group Army includes 196th Infantry Division (Tianjin); 67th Group Army is said to be of uncertain loyalty; 1st Tank Division was moved to Beijing before 3/4 June to support 6th Tank Division.

Small Arms and Other Weapons of the People's Liberation Army

Using extracted data from *Jane's Infantry Weapons 1988/89*, the following catalogue of firepower is presented to enable the reader to more readily identify weaponry discussed in the preceeding essays. Essentially, every PLA soldier has a personal weapon, usually of the AK-47 type and many non-commissioned and commissioned officers carry pistols. At platoon, company and battalion level, support weapons will also be found, although there is very little evidence to support rumours of their use in Tiananmen Square.

Pistols

7.62 mm Type 54 pistol
This is a direct copy of the Soviet 7.62 mm Tokarev TT33 pistol and is the standard pistol in the Chinese Army. It has a semi-automatic recoil action which is fed from an eight-round box magazine.

7.65 mm Type 64 and Type 67 silenced pistols
The Type 64 is a pistol produced solely in silenced form. It may be used either as a manually-operated single-shot weapon or as a self-loader. It can be operated in single-shot or semi-automatic modes, using a nine-round box magazine.

Sub-machine Guns

7.62mm Types 43 and 50 sub-machine gun
The Chinese authorities turned to the Soviet Union for supplies during the Korean War and were provided with the Soviet PPSh-41 sub-machine

The 9 mm machine pistol is a new weapon in the PLA inventory which combines the light weight of a pistol with the automatic fire capability of a sub-machine gun.

gun and the PPS-43. The Chinese subsequently manufactured the PPSh-41 as the Type 50 sub-machine gun. This differs from the Soviet-produced gun only in the markings. The PPS-43 was manufactured in China and known as the Type 43 copy sub-machine gun. Again the only difference between the Soviet and the Chinese weapons is in the markings.

7.62 mm light sub-machine gun Type 85
The Type 85 is a modified and simplified version of the Type 79. There is a folding butt and the weapon uses the same 30-round box magazine as the Type 79.

7.62mm Type 64 silenced sub-machine gun
This is a Chinese-designed and constructed sub-machine gun which combines a number of features taken from various European weapons. The bolt action is the same as that of the Type 43 copy sub-machine gun which was taken from the Soviet

PPS-43. The trigger mechanism, giving selective fire, was taken from the British Bren gun, numbers of which fell into Chinese hands during the Korean War.

7.62 mm Type 85 silenced sub-machine gun
This is a simplified and lightened version of the silenced Type 64 sub-machine gun, produced principally for export. It appears to be based on the simple mechanism of the Type 85 light sub-machine gun, but is of about the same size as the Type 64 and uses similar silencing arrangements. It uses a 30-round box magazine.

Carbines and Assault Rifles

7.62 mm Type 56 carbine
This is a Chinese copy of the Soviet Simonov SKS self-loading carbine. The ten-round, semi-automatic rifle may be identified by the Chinese symbols on the left front of the receiver. The

The Type 79 light sub-machine gun is the forerunner of the Type 85 and is widely used by the PLA and Militia forces. The weapon is simple to use and can be fired by anyone familiar with the handling of the AK-47 without further training.

weapon is fashioned and functions in exactly the same way as the SKS. Later versions of the Type 56 have a spike bayonet replacing the folding blade of conventional shape used on all other SKS variants. It is believed to be in service with reserve units only.

7.62 mm Types 56, 56-1 and 56-2 assault rifles
The Type 56 assault rifle is a copy of the later model of the Soviet AK-47 and is believed to have been used extensively by the 27th Group Army in Tiananmen Square. It can kill at 300 m.

There is also a Type 56-1 assault rifle which has a folding metal stock. The Type 56-2 generally resembles the 56-1 but has a butt stock which folds sideways to lie along the right side of the receiver.

7.62 mm Type 68 rifle
This weapon is of Chinese design and manufacture.

In general appearance it resembles the Type 56 (SKS) carbine but the barrel is longer, the bolt action is based on that of the AK-47 and the rifle provides selective fire. A 15-round detachable box magazine is the standard feed but the 30-round box magazine from the AK-47 can also be used with slight modification. With single shot selected it has an effective range of 400 m and can kill at 200 m on automatic fire.

7.62 mm Type 79 sniping rifle
This rifle is a precise copy of the Soviet SVD Dragunov sniping rifle, except that the butt is slightly shorter. It is equipped with an optical sight which is a copy of the Soviet PSO-1 and has the same ability to detect infra-red emissions. It has an effective range of 800 m.

Types 53, 54, 56 and 58 machine guns are believed

The Type 56 assault rifle is a copy of the later model of the Soviet AK-47. It is fitted with a folding bayonet which hinges down and back to lie beneath the fore-end. It was used extensively by the 27th Group Army in Tiananmen Square.

to be manufactured in China. All appear to remain in service although some are probably used only by reserve units, the People's Militia or the People's Armed Police.

Machine Guns

7.62 mm Type 67 light machine gun
The type 67 is an indigenous Chinese design and has replaced the Types 53 and 58 in front-line units. Of a basically sturdy design, it is strong and reliable although a little heavy. It has been in production since the early 1970s and some of the early issues were given to North Vietnam. The gun is belt-fed and may be used with either a bipod or a tripod for sustained fire to 800 m.

7.62 mm Type 74 light machine gun
This is a platoon light machine gun which is fed from a 101-round drum magazine; it is also possible to use the Type 56 rifle magazine in place of the drum. It appears to be an entirely new design and not simply a re-engineered Kalashnikov. Its effective range is 600 m.

7.62 mm PK style light machine gun
This weapon has only recently been seen in Chinese service. A direct copy of the Soviet PK, it is belt-fed although it can use a belt-box. It has a maximum range of 1000 m.

12.7 mm anti-aircraft machine gun Type 77
The Type 77 is an automatic weapon of new design which is primarily intended for air defence, though it can also be used against ground targets to a maximum range of 1500 m.

12.7 mm anti-aircraft machine gun Type W-85
This is a new design of automatic machine-gun principally intended for use against aerial targets

A Chinese copy of a Soviet PKS light machine gun. The PKS has a rate of fire of 700 rounds of 7.62 mm ammunition a minute to a range of 1000 m.

but which can also be used as a heavy support machine gun against ground targets.

14.5 mm anti-aircraft machine gun Type 75-1
This is a Chinese version of the Soviet KPV machine gun. It is mounted on a tripod with two small wheels, the tripod folding to become a lightweight trailer.

Anti-tank Weapons

Red Arrow 8 guided weapon system
The Red Arrow 8 guided weapon system is a second-generation guided missile intended for use by infantry against tanks and other armoured targets with a range of 100 to 3000 m. It is a crew-portable weapon, fired from a ground tripod mount; it can also be configured for mounting in a variety of wheeled and tracked vehicles.

In general appearance the system is similar to the Anglo-Franco-German Milan anti-tank missile, having a sight unit on to which the missile transport and launch tube is attached before firing.

40 mm Type 56 anti-tank grenade launcher
This is a copy of the Soviet RPG-2 launcher and has the same weight and dimensions. It fires the Type 50 grenade which has better penetration than the Soviet PG-2 high explosive anti-tank (HEAT) round. This weapon is known to be used by the Militia and is presumably in reserve service only.

40 mm Type 69 anti-tank grenade launcher
This is a copy of the Soviet RPG-7 launcher and was not seen until 1972. It has the same performance as the Soviet version.

57 mm Type 36 recoilless rifle
This is a copy of the US M18A1 and is a breech loading single-shot weapon using a high explosive

A 40 mm Type 69 anti-tank grenade launcher. The second crew member has a spare grenade in his hand ready to load and others on his back.

anti-tank round against armour and a high explosive or canister round against personnel. This weapon is probably only in service with the reserve forces of the PLA.

75 mm Type 52 recoilless rifle

This is a copy of the obsolete US M20 recoilless rifle. It offers no improvements over the US Army version and can fire either Chinese or US ammunition.

62 mm portable rocket launcher

This is a man-portable launcher similar in principle to the US M72 light anti-armour weapon. It consists of a telescoping tubular launcher into which a rocket is pre-assembled. The unit is carried in the telescoped condition and extended prior to firing; extending the launch tube automatically cocks the firing mechanism. After firing the launcher is discarded.

Hand Grenades

The People's Liberation Army uses a variety of grenades of both Chinese and Soviet manufacture. The Chinese grenades are similar in design to the Soviet models, except that in most cases they have different dimensions and, as the same design is often made by a number of factories, there are minor differences between copies of the same type of grenade.

Type 42 (offensive/defensive) hand grenade

This is a direct copy of the Soviet RG-42 grenade and it is filled with pressed TNT explosive for an effective fragmentation radius of 15 m.

Type 1 (defensive) hand grenade

This is a copy of the Soviet F1 grenade and uses

cast TNT for an effective fragmentation radius of 15 m.

Type 59 (defensive) hand grenade

This is similar in design to the Soviet RGD-5 grenade and is more powerful than previously described types; it has an effective fragmentation radius of 20 m.

Stick grenades

The Chinese have manufactured a wide variety of stick grenades for defensive operations and it is possible that some of these were used in the opening stages of the clearance of Tiananmen Square. Scored, serrated and plain types have been encountered on other 'battlefields'. Their contents have included picric acid, mixtures of TNT or nitroglycerin with potassium nitrate or sawdust and schneiderite.

The standard method of operation is that the cord of the pull- friction fuze, which is underneath the cap at the end of the throwing handle, is pulled. This ignites the delay element which lasts between 2.5 and 5 seconds, after which the detonator explodes the main charge. These grenades are generally packed in boxes of twenty already fuzed.

This typical example of a defensive stick grenade is known to be still in use. It is a fragmenting type with a serrated head made of grey cast iron. This produces a small number of large fragments and a very large number of fragments so small that they could well be described as 'dust'. The filling is picric acid which was discarded as an explosive filling in the West many years ago, principally because it forms dangerous and unstable compounds. It is essential that the inside of the carrying container is varnished in order to prevent the entrance of moisture which may cause the filling to become unstable.

China's Nuclear Potential

The question being asked around the defence intelligence community immediately after the Tiananmen Square crisis is: Who's got their finger on the nuclear button?

The answer is apparently very simple. During the so-called Cultural Revolution period, China's armed forces, including their nuclear component — the Second Artillery Force — remained aloof from the political antics of the Red Guards. This precedent has been carried over into the present crisis and informed sources believe that China's strategic forces have not been involved in the internal situation.

However, today China's nuclear-capable ground, sea and air nuclear elements, the Strategic Nuclear Command as the Second Artillery Force as it is better known in the West, is a separate military authority under the direction and control of the Minister of Defence. During the 1960s, nuclear weapons were in the hands of the Army General Staff but since then the Navy has developed sea-going strategic systems.

This fourth major military command echelon is also composed of forces, corps, and special elements — submarine, strategic rocket and aviation. Its nuclear weapon inventory is believed to consist of about 1455 devices, both strategic and tactical. The Chinese nuclear arsenal is estimated to consist of 354 strategic systems capable of carrying about 930 warheads; at least 150 land and sea-based tactical missiles along with some 375 deployable munitions.

The United States and the Soviet Union's implementation of the Intermediate-range Nuclear Forces (INF) agreement to eliminate nuclear weapon launchers in the 500 to 5500 km range, coupled with announced trends in START (Strategic Arms Reduction Talks), significantly expands the international importance of China's arsenal. It may well provide China with a near monopoly in the intermediate range class, particularly with nuclear payloads.

The employment of tactical nuclear weapons is considered by a number of Chinese military leaders to be a 'modernised version of forward defence' and that 'miniaturised' enhanced radiation warheads suit battlefield requirements for limited and localised 'self-defence' conflicts.

Contrary to assumed perceptions, China has developed a unique nuclear strategy based upon their age-old strategic tradition — 'integrated deterrence'. In all probability this strategy may be focused more upon the attitudes of probable opponent's strategic planning personnel than upon a country's important physical targets.

The scope of China's current strategic planning goes beyond land, sea, and air to the fourth

China's first atomic bomb was detonated on 16 October 1964.

China claims to have successfully launched its first nuclear missile on 27 October 1966, probably from a launching site in the Gobi desert. The missile is thought to be an experimental forerunner of the CSS-1.

negotiations underway in several nations for Chinese industry to provide the new M series of short-range, road mobile, solid propellant, single warhead missiles.

Development of the M series began in the early 1980s and the design includes the ability to use either high explosive or nuclear warheads. These missiles will probably enter service in the 1990s.

Of the older missiles in service, the CSS-1 (a US designation) intermediate-range system has been deployed in Northern China with a range of 1200 km (capable of striking at Soviet targets) and the CSS-2, which also entered service in the early 1970s and a greater range at 3000km.

In the intercontinental missile arena, the CSS-3, which incorporated substantial Chinese technology for the first time, was the subject of near cancellation during the so-called Cultural Revolution. According to Chinese sources, the missile has been in service with the Second Artillery Corps since the late 1970s and in 1985 was upgraded with new Chinese software. The Long March space launcher is the civil version of this system.

Deployed in hardened silos since 1980-81, the

Part of the civil space programme launch facility from where China launched its first successful commercial satellite in April 1970. The rocket is the Long March 1, which is based on the CSS-3 intercontinental ballistic missile.

dimension of space. Contrary to China pronouncements that Soviet and US strategic defence initiatives are destabilising, an attempt to expand its strategic nuclear force triad into a nuclear deterrent 'self defence' tetrad could well become a major national effort for the 1990s.

China is also one of 16 nations identified in *Jane's Strategic Weapon Systems* which is claimed to have the capability to produce short-range ballistic missiles. In 1988, the Chinese sold the CSS-2 missile, with a 1500 km range, to Saudi Arabia as part of that nation's first strategic deterrence posture. China has also been accused of providing technical information to other members of the Third World ballistic missile club, including

CSS-4 intercontinental range ballistic missile, known as Dong Feng (East Wind) to the Chinese, has a range of 10 000km and carries a 1 to 5 megaton nuclear warhead. Twenty such missiles are thought to have been deployed and the deployment of the missile may have been one of the reasons for the decision by the Soviet Union to upgrade the ballistic missile defences around Moscow.

Western sources have been able to identify two naval strategic weapon systems in the last ten years. The CSS-N-3 is an intermediate range (about 2700km) submarine-launched ballistic missile with a two megaton warhead. The missiles were ceremonially paraded in Beijing in October 1984 and it is believed that they became operational in 1986. The *Xia* class submarine is the host vessel and 24 missiles have been embarked.

In late 1985, the Liberation Army Journal announced that a new submarine-launched nuclear capable ballistic missile was being developed for future *Xia* class submarines. The new craft will carry 16 missiles each but very little else is known about the missile or its operational status.

Estimated PRC Nuclear Weapon Inventory — 1989

According to US reports, China has a total of 1455 warheads[a.] with yields in the two kilotonne to five megatonne range.

Category	System Designation	IOC	Range 1000 km	Number: Missiles/ Aircraft	Potential Warheads/ Missile	Total
Land-based						
ICBM(fr)	DF-7/CZ-4/CCS-6?[b.]	1989	15	1+	3	3
ICBM(er)	DF-6/CZ-3A/CSS-5?[c.]	1984	19	5	10	50
ICBM(fr)	DF-5/CZ-2D/CSS-4[d.]	1975	13	25	10	250
ICBM(lr)	DF-4/CZ-1C/CSS-3[e.]	1973	10	35	3	105
IRBM	DF-3/T-3/CSS-2[f.]	1972	3.2	20	1	20
	Improved DF-3	1983	5.5	80	3	240
MRBM	DF-2/T-2/CSS-1	1966	1.8	60	1	60
SRBM[g.]	Modified DF-1/T-5	1978	0.1	100	1TNW	100
	M-series(9/11)	1987/8	0.6/.1	25	1TNW	25
Artillery[h.]	S23-type 152/203 mm (nuclear shells)	1979?	0.025	100	1TNW	100
Munitions	(nuclear mines)	1964	–	25	1	25
Sea-based						
SLBM	JL-1/CSS-N-3[i.]	1982	?4	36	3	100
SLCM	SY-3?	1987	?	16	1	16
SLSM	SY-4?[k.]	1989	?	1+	3	3
SRCM	HY-2 series [l.]	1980	0.04-9	25	1TNW	25
Munitions[m.]	(nuclear torpedos) and depth charges)	1980	–	25	1	25
Air-launched						
ALCM[n.]	C-601	1987	0.16	50	1	50
	HY-4	1985	0.135	25	1	25
Bomb[o.]	Hong 6 medium bomber	1966	4.8	50	1	50
	Hong 7 fighter/bomber	1988	3.0?	5	1	5
	Qiang 5 attack	1978	2.2	100	1	100
	Jian 8B/II strike	1984/88	2.2	70	ITNW	70

China is thought to have developed nuclear artillery shells for the 203 mm weapon system. Smaller calibres are probably not available as the technology needed to produce such a small, concentrated round for the 155 mm round has not been developed yet. It is certain that neither the USA not the UK will provide that level of technology to China following Tiananmen Square.

Abbreviations:

CZ	–	Chang Zheng (Long March)
DF	–	Dong Feng (East Wind)
FL	–	Fei Lung (Flying Dragon)
JL	–	Ju Lang (Giant Wave)
HY	–	Hai Ying (Sea Eagle)
SY	–	Shui Ying (Water Eagle)
ALCM	–	Air Launched Cruise Missile
ICBM(er)	–	Intercontinental Ballistic Missile, extended range
ICBM (fr)	–	Intercontinental Ballistic Missile, full range
ICBM(lr)	–	Intercontinental Ballistic Missile, limited range
IRBM	–	Intermediate Range Ballistic Missile
MIRV	–	Multiple Independant Reentry Vehicle
MRBM	–	Medium Range Ballistic Missile
SLBM	–	Submaine Launched Ballistic Missile
SLCM	–	Submarine Launched Cruise Missile
SLSM	–	Ship Launched Strategic Missile
SRBM	–	Short range Ballistic Missile
SRCM	–	Short range Cruise Missile
TNW	–	Tactical Nuclear Weapon

Notes:

a. A high ranking Chinese official claimed in June 1985 that the USA and the USSR possesses 95 per cent of all the world's nuclear weaponry. Another reported that the combined total was 43 990 weapons of all types placing China in third place. Assuming 2 per cent for the United Kingdom, France, and India combined, China's 3 per cent of a world total based upon the aforementioned 95 percentage figure, would be 1390 nuclear warheads. Based upon a previously reported production rate of 70 new warheads annually, China could have produced about 1490 nuclear explosive devices. An estimated 23 550kg of weapon grade U235 and Pu239 has been produced since 1962, an average of 16kg per warhead (about 5kg of Pu239 is required to make a 20KT warhead). Allowing for the known detonation of 34 warheads during testing and training exercises some 1455 remain.

b. The DF-7 is the military version of the new CZ-4 three stage missile capable of launching a 1.5 tonne spacecraft into a sun synchronous orbit.

c. Presuming and annual production rate of six DF-6/CZ-3 boosters since 1984, up to 18 three-stage carrier rockets could have been produced, four of which have been used to place communication satellites into geo-synchronous orbit. Another was test-launched by the PLA. Allowing that two-thirds of the remainder have been assigned to civilian or commercial space activities, some five DF-6 rockets should be available to the strategic rocket forces.

d. At least 25FB-1/DF-5/CZ-3-type carrier rockets have been launched since 1971. Production rate for this two-stage liquid fuel booster has been estimated at 6 per year since the early 1980s. Assuming that one-third of those produced since 1983 were utilised by the civilian space programme, more than 20 missiles could have gone into military inventories. As a result of continuing technology advances, the initial 5MT yield fusion warhead weight has been step-reduced from 5 tonnes and 3.8 tonnes to 3.2 tonnes, respectively.

e. The initial production series of the DF-3 missile were fitted with a single 1+ megatonne yield, 1.5 megatonne warhead. Since a DF-4 missile utilises the DF-3 as its first stage, DF-3 missiles can readily be transformed into DF-4s should strategic situations demand it. The CZ-1 launch system is a modified DF-4 with a third stage.

f. During September 1984, an improved DF-3 IRBM fitted with a MIRV nose cone, was successfully test-fired from the Xichang launch complex near Chengdu in south-west China. This MIRV nose-cone and the one fitted to a DF-5 ICBM appear very similar.

g. A senior PLA Navy officer advised that China, as the result of a number of significant technological accomplishments, now has the capability to launch tactical nuclear missiles. The new SST M-series missiles are designed to be battlefield support weapons. The M-9 (SST-600) is a 9-metre long, 600 km range, solid fuel, inertially guided, rocket deployed and

An Eagle Strike missile launched from a Modified Romeo *class cruise missile conventionally-powered submarine, designated ES5G by the PLA Navy. The submarine is capable of carrying six C-801 missiles which are considered to be second generation sea skimmers. Sources say that there is a potential for a smll nuclear warhead to be carried.*

launched from a multi-functional 4-axle cross-country vehicle. The M-11, having a range of about 135 km is similarly deployed. Both the M-9 and M-11 rockets, fitted with either a high explosive or low yield tactical (possibly enhanced radiation) nuclear warhead, are designed to be employed against slowly moving targets, troop concentration, tank formations, communication centres, air defence positions, ammunition depots, parked aircraft and missile launching sites.

h. Reportedly the 203 mm nuclear artillery shell reportedly has a yield of 5 kilotonnes and the 152 mm nuclear artillery shell a yield of 1 kilotonne. The PLA Army artillery inventory consists of 400 203 mm and 700 152 mm artillery pieces. Command of Tactical Nuclear Artillery is an independent hierarchy. Prior to the recent reorganisation of the PLA some 90 artillery battalions from 20 field artillery divisions were deployed along the East Sea coast and Soviet border areas.

i. Assuming a full complement of 12 JL-1 missiles aboard each of the two or three operational *Xia* class SSBNs.

j. On 28 September 1985, the PLA Navy conducted its first operational test-launch of an

High ranking PLA naval officers have indicated that China would like a surface ship-launched nuclear missile and the Jianghu V class destroyers are possible carriers. This type is already equipped with HY-2 Silkworm and C-801 Eagle Strike missiles.

intermediate range nuclear capable submarine launched cruise missile (SLCM) from a submarine operating in Western Pacific waters to a target about 480 km from Taiwan..

k. A high-level PLA Navy official recently claimed that China is developing a new ship-based strategic missile. This could be the new missile recently fabricated by the Xinzhonghua Factory, Shanghai. According to the *Xinhua News* agency, the rocket is scheduled for testing in the near future.

l. The Minghe-type SSMs (FL/HY series), aerodynamic tactical missiles are capable of being fitted with up to a 20 kilotonne size nuclear warhead. The FL series (Fei Lung/Flying Dragon) SSMs are sea launched. The HY (Hai Ying/Sea Eagle) series are anti-ship weapons fired from land mobile launchers.

m. Unconfirmed reports suggest the PLA Navy may possess a limited number of Hong-6 launched nuclear depth charges and submarine launched 533 mm diameter nuclear-tipped torpedoes, both weapons system designs are believed to be based upon USSR technology.

n. The C-601 is a high subsonic, air launched, nuclear-capable cruise missile. Two can be deployed by a Hong-6D bomber. From a launch-altitude of 9000 metres, a range of 160km can be obtained. Similarly launched the HY-4, also a subsonic nuclear — capable cruise missile, can reach a range of about 135 km.

o. Assuming an availability of one bomb per aircraft. An estimated 80 per cent of low-yield nuclear warheads are fitted to bombs because delivery method provides great manoeuvrability and operational radius. According to several Chinese officials the B-7 twin-jet fighter/bomber aircraft, which reached a speed of Mach 1.75 at an altitude of 11 000 metres, has successfully completed all technical qualification trials. First production units from Xian Aircraft Works began entering operational service during November 1988. This aircraft design is being produced in both the Air Force and Navy version. Principle differences (external at least) appear to be related to weapon deployment. The aircraft is equipped with an all-weather attack and terrain-following radar system. The Q-5 fighter-bomber is capable of delivering 10 kilotonne nuclear bombs.

The Xian H-6 medium bomber is capable of carrying both conventional and nuclear bombs, as well as the C-601 missile manufactures by CPMIEC in Beijing.

Inventory of the PLA

PERSONNEL

Army:	2 300 000
Navy:	300 000
Air Force:	380 000
Total Military	2 980 000

Army Reserves:

It is understood that prior to the recent unrest, the reserves were being re-organised and possibly reduced in size. No figures for the planned reductions have been released. Previous estimates have been 12 million.

Men and women between the ages of 18-28 with previous military experience are expected to serve in the People's Militia. This force is estimated to be about 4.3 million strong. The recently formed People's Armed Police have a reported strength of about 5 million, according to some sources.

STRATEGIC NUCLEAR FORCES

Personnel in the fourth arm of the PLA, also known as the Second Artillery or the Strategic Rocket Forces, number about 90 000.

Naval systems:

CSS-N-3 submarine-launched missile with 2MT warhead
(12 carried on China's two or three operational SSBNs)

Land-based systems:

CSS-1 medium range ballistic missiles (50) 15 or 20KT warhead
CSS-2 intermediate range ballistic missiles (60); 3MT warhead
CSS-3 intercontinental ballistic missiles (30) 2MT warhead
CSS-4 intercontinental ballistic missiles (10) 5MT warhead

Air systems:

Some of China's 120 Xian H-6 medium bombers may be nuclear-capable, using free-fall bombs. US sources also maintain that the Eagle Strike missile is capable of carrying a nuclear warhead.

PLA EQUIPMENT

Main Battle Tanks

Sources give figures of between 8000 and 9000 for the total number of MBTs, including about 6000 Type 59 and Type 69 models. There are also unkown numbers of Type 79 and Type 80 in service. In addition, there are a number of older variants, including T-34s. The latter types are still production for the PLA .

Light Tanks

About 1200 Type 62 and some 800 Type 63 variants are in service; the latter is still in production.

Armoured Personnel Carriers

Estimates for the number of APCs in the PLA vary considerably, but it is thought that at least 12 000 are in service. That number includes the Types 501, 77, 534, 551, 531 and 523. These figures include the command post, ambulance, recovery and other specialist variants.

Self-Propelled Artillery

The PLA operates three types of SP artillery, the Types 83 (152 mm), 85 and 54-1 (122 mm); all three remain in production.

Self-Propelled Anti-Aircraft Artillery

China has developed the Type 80 twin 57 mm system which is already in production and the Type 69 Mod system (twin 37 mm) which was declared ready for production in 1987. Exact numbers in service are unknown.

Towed Artillery

Large numbers of guns remain in service with the PLA (it should be remembered that there are more troops in the artillery regiments than serving as infantrymen). The largest calibre is the 152 mm (Types 54 and 66), although US sources say that there are nuclear-capable 203mm The latest 130mm system is the Type 59-1 which has replaced the Type 59 in service. Two 122 mm field howitzer systems are the Types 54-1 and D-30, whilst the Types 86 and 56 make up the remaining system at 100 mm. It is understood that the Type 56 85 mm field gun is in limited service.

Multiple Rocket Launchers

The PLA has a large number of rocket launchers varying from the Type 762 425 mm mine-clearing rocket (about 1000 systems), through the 10-round Type 74 multiple 284 mm minelaying rocket system, the Type 83 (273 mm) multiple rocket launcher, the 130 mm Types 63, 70 and 82 rocket systems to the new 122mm systems. The Type 81 122 mm system is still in production and services alongside the Type 83. Lower down the scale, there are large numbers of Type 63 and Type 81 107 mm rocket launcher systems, but again exact figures are impossible to obtain.

Mortars

The largest mortar system in the PLA is the 160 mm Type 56 which is supported by a self-propelled 120 mm (WZ381) and several other towed/carried variants of the same calibre. At 82 mm and 100 mm there are many thousands of Type 53 and Type 71 mortars respectively.

Anti-Tank Guided Weapons

The H-8 has been designed in China but bears a striking resemblance to the Milan system. It is estimated that there are some 20 000 anti-tank guided weapon launchers available to the PLA Army.

Anti-Tank Unguided Weapons

Two 40 mm grenade launchers are in service, the Types 56 and 69. The standard discardable system is a portable 62mm rocket.

Recoiless launchers

Unknown numbers of Type 36 57 mm recoiless rifles, Type 52 75 mm recoiless rifles, Type 65 82 mm guns and Type 75 105 mm self-propelled.

Rocket Launchers

Large numbers of 90 mm Type 51 launchers are in service.

Anti-tank Guns

The standard systems are 57 mm (Type 55), 76 mm (Type 54) and 100 mm (Type 73).

Air Defence — Guns

There are about 15 000 anti-tank guns in service, ranging from 100 mm to 12.7 mm weapons. Demountable guns were seen in Beijing during the Tiananmen Square.

Air Defence — SAMs

There are 100 HQ-2J missiles and a number of other systems are in service. Several are thought to be copies of Soviet systems.

Army Aviation

Recently, an army aviation corps has been formed to provide integral battlefield helicopter support to the Group Armies and the independent divisions. In addition, the Garrison commanders have their own helicopter liaision. Leaflets were dropped on Tiananmen Square during the immediate post-Martial Law period by local Garrison Aerospatiale SA 342L Gazelle helicopters. These helicopters, thought to number 20 can also carry HOT anti-tank missiles and are capable of night vision goggle operations.

AIR FORCE INVENTORY

Latest estimates give the air force inventory as 6000 combat aircraft.

Interceptor Aircraft
Shenyang J-5 'Fresco'   400

Shenyang J-6 'Farmer'   800
Xian J-7 'Fishbed' 500
Shenyang J-8 'Finback' 130

Strike
Nanchang Q-5   500
Shenyang J-4 'Fresco'   250
Shenyang J-5 'Fresco'   500
Shenyang J-6 'Farmer'   1200
Shenyang J-8II 'Finback'20

Medium Bombers
Xian H-6   120

Light Bombers
Shenyang H-5 'Beagle'   400

Reconnaissance
Shenyang HZ-5 'Beagle' 50
Shenyang JZ-6 'Farmer' 80

Transport Aircaft
BAe Trident 15
Canadair CL-601 Challenger   3
Ilyushin IL-14   36
Ilyushin IL-18   10
Shijiazuang Y-5   300
Tupolev Tu-124   1
Xian Y-7 (An-24) 60
Xian Y-8 (An-12) 50

Trainer Aircaft
Shenyang JJ-6   600
Other types include the Nancheng CJ-5, CJ-6,
Shenyang HJ-5, JJ-2, JJ-5 and JJ-6, but no reliable
figures are available.

Helicopters
Aerospatiale SA 319B Alouette III   50
Aerospatiale AS 332M Super Puma   6
Aerospatiale SA 321JA Super Frelon 10
Aerospatiale SA 365N Dauphin 9
Harbin Z-5 'Hound'   300
Harbin Z-6 'Hip'   100
Harbin Z-9A (Dauphin) 20
Bell 214ST 4
Boeing CH-47D Chinook   20*
Sikorsky S-70C   24

NAVAL AIRCRAFT

Embarked aircraft
Aerospatiale SA 321G Super Frelon   13
Harbin Z-8 (Super Frelon)   2
Harbin Z-9A (Dauphin) 10 (40)*

Shore-based aircraft
Beriev Be-6 'Madge'   12
Hanzhong Y-8   1
Harbin H-5 'Beagle'   80
Harbin Z-5 'Hound'   40
Nanchang JZ-5   40
Nanchang JZ-6   30
Nanchang Q-5 'Fantail' 100
Shenyang J-5 'Fresco'   150
Shenyang J-6 'Farmer'   300
Shenyang JJ-2 'Mongul' 20
Shenyang JJ-5/JJ-6   150
Tupolev Tu-16/Xian H-6 'Badger'   35
Xian J-7 'Fishbed' 200

* denotes aircraft to be delivered.